APPLICATION SUPPORT INTERVIEWS QUESTIONS IN INVESTMENT BANK

Question 1. How Do you troubleshoot once your application is not working? Reported by the user.

Answer: During investigating the issue we need to take care following points

First Log the incident with details on how many users impacted. Error details with the primary investigation

Communication to the users and management (Based on Incident Priority)

Based on application architecture investigation for the logs (Web, App, Database servers)

Once we identify error and solution for the issue then fix the issue.

Provide Root cause analysis to all stakeholders

Question 2. What is Incident management process. How do you Prioritize any incident or issues in Application Support?

Answer: Incident Management aims to manage the lifecycle of all Incidents (unplanned interruptions or reductions in quality of IT services). The primary objective of this ITIL process is to return the IT service to users as quickly as possible.

ITIL distinguishes between Incidents (service interruptions) and Service Requests (customer or user requests that do not represent a service disruption, such as a password reset). Service interruptions are handled through Incident Management, and Service Requests through Request Fulfilment.

ITIL Incident Management

The Incident Management process can be triggered in various ways: A user, customer or supplier may report an issue, technical staff may notice a (potential or actual) failure, or an Incident may be raised automatically by an event monitoring system.

All Incidents should be logged as Incident Records, where their status can be tracked, and a complete historical record maintained. Initial categorization and prioritization of Incidents is a critical step for determining how the Incident will be handled and how much time is available for its resolution (see checklist Incident Prioritization Guideline).

If possible, Incidents should be matched to other Incidents, Problems and Known Errors.

Organizations should use automated resolution tools and provide support portals with self-help information so users can resolve simple Incidents themselves. For other Incidents, 1st Level Support will try to diagnose and resolve the issue, typically using information from a knowledge base or pre-defined Incident

Models.

If 1st Level Support is unable to resolve an Incident, it must be escalated to an appropriate specialist support group in 2nd Level Support ("functional escalation"). If required, 2nd Level Support may in turn involve external parties such as suppliers and vendors (in ITIL referred to as "3rd Level Support").

ITIL defines a special process for dealing with Major Incidents (emergencies that affect business-critical services and require immediate attention). Major Incidents typically require a temporary Major Incident Team to identify and implement the resolution.

Once Incidents are resolved, 1st Level Support will formally close them. This includes verifying that the users are satisfied and ensuring that the Incident Record is fully documented (see Incident Closure and Evaluation). Any new Problems, Workarounds or Known Errors identified during Incident resolution should be forwarded to the Problem Management process.

Incident Management interfaces with a number of other ITIL processes:

Question 3. What is the Disaster recovery process and how you will handle it?

Answer: A disaster recovery plan (DRP) is a documented process or set of procedures to execute an organization's disaster recovery processes and recover and protect a business IT infrastructure in the event of a disaster. It is "a comprehensive statement of consistent actions to be taken before, during, and after a disaster".

Failover: In this event, application servers move from Prod To Contingency environment

Failback: In this event, application servers move from Contingency to Prod environment

Question 4. How do you define SLA and OLA?

Answer: The Service Level Agreement (SLA) is an agreement between an IT service provider and a customer. The Operational Level Agreement (OLA) is an agreement between an IT service provider and another part of the same organization, governing the delivery of infrastructure service.

Question 5. What are the Change Management Process and Different types of changes in Application Support?

Answer: The Change Management process described here follows the specifications of ITIL V3, where Change Management is a process in the service lifecycle stage of Service Transition.

Change Management seeks to minimize the risk associated with Changes, where ITIL defines a Change as "the addition, modification or removal of anything that could have an effect on IT services". This includes changes to the IT infrastructure, processes, documents, supplier interfaces, etc.

ITIL distinguishes between three different types of Changes:

Standard Changes: Pre-authorized, low-risk Changes that follow a well-known procedure.
Emergency Changes: Changes that must be implemented

immediately, for example, to resolve a Major Incident.

Normal Changes: All other Changes that are not Standard Changes or Emergency Changes.

Expedited Changes

Normal Changes are often further categorized as Major, Significant or Minor, depending on the level of risk involved. Organizations should define these types of Changes and the required Change Authorities in their Change Policy. For example, Major Changes may require a full review by the CAB (Change Advisory Board), while Significant Changes may be approved by the Change Manager.

If a Non-Standard Change is needed, the party requiring the Change will typically submit a Request for Change (RFC) to Change Management. Change Management will then record, analyze and approve (or reject) the Change.

Emergency Changes are assessed and approved by the ECAB (Emergency Change Advisory Board), a core group of CAB members that is available on short notice to respond to emergencies.

For certain types of Changes, a formal Change evaluation takes place by the Change Evaluation process and is documented in a Change Evaluation Report.

Question 6. What is the Release Management process and what are the challenges in Application Support?

Answer: Release Management is a process that entails the management, planning, scheduling, and controlling of an entire software build through every stage and environment involved, including testing and deploying software releases.

Release management requires the following details

1.UAT release steps sign off

2.Implementation plan

3.Backout Plan

4.Host and account details

Challenges are given below

Implementation steps not clear
UAT testing was not properly done so issues in Production
The back out plan was not tested so issues

Question 7. What are Job scheduling tools and How the Application Support team need to handle this?

Answer: A job scheduler is a tool for automating IT processes. In most cases, this is done on a platform-by-platform basis. For example, there are many native job schedulers built into operating systems. Microsoft Windows features Windows Task Scheduler, while Linux and UNIX platforms have cron as their native job scheduler.

Autosys

Control M

Tidal

Question 8. What is a Privileged account and how the Application support team needs to handle Privileged accounts?

Answer: A privileged account is a user account that has more privileges than ordinary users. Privileged accounts might, for example, be able to install or remove software, upgrade the operating system, or modify system or application configurations.

Different types of tools used in the bank to handle Privileged accounts

Cyberark

TPAM

Question 9. How to handle communications during major incidents in Application Support?

Answer: During the event, you will learn how to:

Immediately Identify a major incident

Instantly locate available major incident managers and target notifications to them

Get the right resolution team on the job fast based on the required expertise

Utilize one-click conference bridge technology to get key stakeholders together instantly

Conduct reviews to identify improvements and prevent similar incidents from reoccurring

Question 10. What is Problem Management and how that help to resolve issues?

Answer: Problem Management is an IT service management process tasked with managing the life cycle of underlying "Problems." Success is achieved by quickly detecting and providing solutions or workarounds to Problems in order to minimize the impact on the organization and prevent a recurrence.

ORACLE SUPPORT INTERVIEWS PART 1

Oracle support interview is a combination of Oracle Database related questions and SQL related questions. This is in 5 Parts and first Part is shown below

Oracle related questions are given below:

Oracle (PL/SQL) Interview Questions

Question 1: What is DBMS?

Answer: DBMS: A Database Management System (DBMS) is a program that controls creation, maintenance and use of a database. DBMS can be termed as File Manager that manages data in a database rather than saving it in file systems.

The interactions catered for by most existing DBMS fall into four main groups:

Data definition. Defining new data structures for a database, removing data structures from the database, modifying the structure of existing data.

Update. Inserting, modifying, and deleting data.

Retrieval. Obtaining information either for end-user queries and reports or for processing by applications.

Administration. Registering and monitoring users, enforcing data security, monitoring performance, maintaining data integrity, dealing with concurrency control, and recovering information if the system fails.

A DBMS is responsible for maintaining the integrity and security of stored data, and for recovering information if the system fails.

Benefits of DBMS:

Reduce the data redundancy.

Reduce data inconsistencies.

Multiple Access.

Data Integrity (Data accuracy).

Data Security.

Question 2: What is RDBMS?

Answer: RDBMS stands for Relational Database Management System. RDBMS store the data into the collection of tables, which is related by common fields between the columns of the table. It also provides relational operators to manipulate the data stored into the tables.

A relational database management system (RDBMS) is a database management system (DBMS) that is based on the relational model as introduced by E. F. Codd,

Rule 000: A RDBMS system should be capable of using its relational facilities (exclusively) to manage the database.

Rule 1: The information rule : All information in the database is to be represented in one and only one way. This is achieved by values in column positions within rows of tables.

Rule 2 : The guaranteed access rule : All data must be accessible with no ambiguity. This is achieved in the RDBMS by using the primary key concept.

Rule 3: Systematic treatment of null values : The DBMS must allow each field to remain null. The null can be stored in any field of any datatype.

Rule 4: Active online catalog based on the relational model : The authorized users can access the database structure by using common language i.e SQL.

Rule 5: The comprehensive data sublanguage rule: The system must support at least one relational language that has simple syntax and transaction management facilities. It can be used in the application as well as in the RDBMS systems.

Rule 6: The view updating rule: All views must be update able by the system.

Rule 7: High-level insert, update, and delete: The system can insert, update and delete operations fully. It can also perform the operations on multiple rows simultaneously.

Rule 8: Physical data independence: Changes to the physical storage structure must not require a change to an application based on the structure.

Rule 9: Logical data independence: Changes to the logical level (tables, columns, rows, and so on) must not require a change to an application based on the structure.

Rule 10: Integrity independence: All the Integrity constraints like primary key, unique key etc must be specified separately from application programs and stored in the catalogue.

Rule 11: Distribution independence : The distribution of portions of the database to various locations should be invisible to users of the database.

Rule 12: The non subversion rule: If the system provides a low-level (record-at-a-time) interface, then that interface cannot be used to subvert the system, for example, bypassing a relational security or integrity constraint.

Question 3: What is SQL?

Answer: SQL stands for Structured Query Language, and it is used to communicate with the Database. This is a standard language used to perform tasks such as retrieval, update, insertion and deletion of data from a database.

The SQL language is subdivided into several language elements, including:

Clauses, which are constituent components of statements and queries.

Expressions, which can produce either scalar values, or tables consisting of columns and rows of data.

Predicates, which specify conditions that can be evaluated to SQL three-valued logic (3VL) or Boolean(true/false/unknown) truth values and which are used to limit the effects of statements and queries, or to change program flow.

Queries, which retrieve the data based on specific criteria. This is the most important element of SQL.

Statements, which may have a persistent effect on schemata and data, or which may control transactions, program flow, connections, sessions, or diagnostics.

Question 4: What is SQL Queries?

Queries: The most common operation in SQL is the query, which is performed with the declarative SELECT statement. SELECT retrieves data from one or more tables, or expressions.

A query includes a list of columns to be included in the final result immediately following the SELECT keyword. An asterisk ("*") can also be used to specify that the query should return all columns of the queried tables. SELECT is the most complex statement in SQL, with optional keywords and clauses that include:

The FROM clause which indicates the table(s) from which data is to be retrieved. The FROM clause can include optional JOIN sub clauses to specify the rules for joining tables.

The WHERE clause includes a comparison predicate, which restricts the rows returned by the query. The WHERE clause eliminates all rows from the result set for which the comparison predicate does not evaluate to True.

The GROUP BY clause is used to project rows having common values into a smaller set of rows. GROUP BY is often used in conjunction with SQL aggregation functions or to eliminate duplicate rows from a result set. The WHERE clause is applied before the GROUP BY clause.

The HAVING clause includes a predicate used to filter rows resulting from the GROUP BY clause. Because it acts on the results of the GROUP BY clause, aggregation functions can be used in the HAVING clause predicate.

The ORDER BY clause identifies which columns are used to sort the resulting data, and in which direction they should be sorted (options are ascending or descending). Without an ORDER BY clause, the order of rows returned by an SQL query is undefined.

SQL combines the roles of data definition, data manipulation, and query in a single language. It was one of the first commercial languages for the relational model, although it departs in some respects from the relational model as described by Codd (for example, the rows and columns of a table can be ordered).

Question 5: What is DDL?

Answer: Data Definition Language (DDL): It's a set of SQL commands used to create modify and delete database structures but not the data. DDL manages table and index structure. The most basic items of DDL are CREATE, ALTER, RENAME, DROP and TRUNCATE statements:

CREATE creates an object (a table, for example) in the database, e.g.:

CREATE TABLE My_table(my_field1 INT, my_field2 VARCHAR(50), my_field3 DATE NOT NULL, PRIMARY KEY (my_field1, my_field2));

ALTER modifies the structure of an existing object in various ways, for example, adding a column to an existing table or a constraint, e.g.:

ALTER TABLE My_table ADD my_field4 NUMBER(3) NOT NULL;

TRUNCATE deletes all data from a table in a very fast way, deleting the data inside the table and not the table itself. It usually implies a subsequent COMMIT operation, i.e., it cannot be rolled back (data is not written to the logs for rollback later, unlike DELETE).

TRUNCATE TABLE My_table;

DROP deletes an object in the database, usually irretrievably, i.e., it cannot be rolled back, e.g.:

DROP TABLE My_table;

Question 6: What is DML?

Answer: Data manipulation The Data Manipulation Language (DML) is the subset of SQL used to add, update and delete data:

INSERT adds rows (formally tuples) to an existing table, e.g.:

INSERT INTO My_table (field1, field2, field3)

VALUES ('test', 'N', NULL);

UPDATE modifies a set of existing table rows, e.g.:

UPDATE My_table SET field1 = 'updated value' WHERE field2 = 'N';

DELETE removes existing rows from a table, e.g.:

DELETE FROM My_table WHERE field2 = 'N';

MERGE is used to combine the data of multiple tables. It combines the INSERT and UPDATE elements.

MERGE INTO TABLE_NAME USING table_reference ON (condition)

WHEN MATCHED THEN

UPDATE SET column1 = value1 [, column2 = value2 ...]

WHEN NOT MATCHED THEN

INSERT (column1 [, column2 ...]) VALUES (value1 [, value2 ...])

Question 7: What are Transaction Controls?

Transaction controls: It is component of SQL statement that control access to data. Transactions, if available, wrap DML operations:

START TRANSACTION (or BEGIN WORK, or BEGIN TRANSACTION, depending on SQL dialect) marks the start of a database transaction, which either completes entirely or not at all.

SAVE TRANSACTION (or SAVE POINT) saves the state of the database at the current point in transaction

CREATE TABLE tbl_1(id INT);

INSERT INTO tbl_1(id) VALUES(1);

INSERT INTO tbl_1(id) VALUES(2);

COMMIT;

UPDATE tbl_1 SET id=200 WHERE id=1;

SAVEPOINT id_1upd;

UPDATE tbl_1 SET id=1000 WHERE id=2;

ROLLBACK TO id_1upd;

SELECT id FROM tbl_1;

COMMIT causes all data changes in a transaction to be made permanent.

ROLLBACK causes all data changes since the last COMMIT or

ROLLBACK to be discarded, leaving the state of the data as it was prior to those changes.

Once the COMMIT statement completes, the transaction's changes cannot be rolled back.

COMMIT and ROLLBACK terminate the current transaction and release data locks. In the absence of a START TRANSACTION or similar statement, the semantics of SQL are implementation dependent. The following example shows a classic transfer of funds transaction, where money is removed from one account and added to another. If either the removal or the addition fails, the entire transaction is rolled back.

START TRANSACTION;

UPDATE Account SET amount=amount-200 WHERE account_number=1234;

UPDATE Account SET amount=amount+200 WHERE account_number=2345;

IF ERRORS=0 COMMIT;

IF ERRORS<>0 ROLLBACK;

Question 8: What is Normalization and why it is used?

Answer: In the design of a relational database management system (RDBMS), the process of organizing data to minimize redundancy is called normalization.

The goal of database normalization is to decompose relations with anomalies in order to produce smaller, well-structured relations. Normalization usually involves dividing large tables into smaller (and less redundant) tables and defining relationships between them. The objective is to isolate data so that additions, deletions, and modifications of a field can be made in just one table and then propagated through the rest of the database via the defined relationships.

Normalization is the process of minimizing redundancy and dependency by organizing fields and table of a database. The main aim of Normalization is to add, delete or modify field that can be made in a single table.

Question 9: What is De normalization.

Answer De Normalization is a technique used to access the data from higher to lower normal forms of database. It is also process of introducing redundancy into a table by incorporating data from the related tables.

Question 10: What are all the different normalization?

Answer The normal forms can be divided into 5 forms, and they are explained below -.

First Normal Form (1NF):.This should remove all the duplicate columns from the table. Creation of tables for the related data and identification of unique columns.

Second Normal Form (2NF): Meeting all requirements of the first normal form. Placing the subsets of data in separate tables and Creation of relationships between the tables using primary keys.

Third Normal Form (3NF): This should meet all requirements of 2NF. Removing the columns which are not dependent on primary key constraints.

Fourth Normal Form (3NF): Meeting all the requirements of third normal form and it should not have multi- valued dependencies.

ORACLE SUPPORT INTERVIEW PART 2

Oracle support interview is a combination of Oracle Database related questions and SQL related questions. This is part of 5 Parts series and second Part is shown below

Oracle related questions are given below:

Oracle (PL/SQL) Interview Questions

Question 1: What is a primary key?

Answer: A primary key is a combination of fields which uniquely specify a row. This is a special kind of unique key, and it has implicit NOT NULL constraint. It means, Primary key values cannot be NULL.

Question 2: What is a unique key?

Answer A Unique key constraint uniquely identified each record in the database. This provides uniqueness for the column or set of columns. A Primary key constraint has automatic unique constraint defined on it. But not, in the case of Unique Key .There can be many unique constraint defined per table, but only one Primary key constraint defined per table.

Question 3: What is a foreign key?

Answer A foreign key is one table which can be related to the primary key of another table. Relationship needs to be created between two tables by referencing foreign key with the primary key of another table.

Question 4: What is an Index?

Answer An index is performance tuning method of allowing faster retrieval of records from the table. An index creates an entry for each value and it will be faster to retrieve data.

Question 5: What are all the different types of indexes?

Answer

Unique Index. This indexing does not allow the field to have duplicate values if the column is unique indexed. Unique index can be applied automatically when primary key is defined.

Clustered Index. This type of index reorders the physical order of the table and search based on the key values. Each table can have only one clustered index.

Non Clustered Index. Non-Clustered Index does not alter the physical order of the table and maintains logical order of data. Each table can have 999 non clustered indexes.

Question 6: What is a join?

Answer: This is a keyword used to query data from more tables based on the relationship between the fields of the tables. Keys play a major role when Joins are used.

Question 7: What are the types of joins and explain each?

Answer There are various types of join which can be used to retrieve data and it depends on the relationship between tables.

Inner join. Inner join return rows when there is at least one match of rows between the tables.

Right Join. Right join return rows which are common between the tables and all rows of Right-hand side table. Simply, it returns all the rows from the right-hand side table even though there are no matches in the left hand side table.

Left Join. Left join return rows which are common between the tables and all rows of Left-hand side table. Simply, it returns all the rows from Left hand side table even though there are no matches in the Right-hand side table.

Full Join. Full join return rows when there are matching rows in any one of the tables. This means, it returns all the rows from the left-hand side table and all the rows from the right hand side table.

Question 8: What is a View?

Answer A view is a virtual table which consists of a subset of data contained in a table. Views are not virtually present, and it takes less space to store. View can have data of one or more tables combined, and it is depending on the relationship.

Question 9. What is a Cursor?

Answer A database Cursor is a control which enables traversal over the rows or records in the table. This can be viewed as a pointer to one row in a set of rows. Cursor is very much useful for traversing such as retrieval, addition and removal of database records.

Question 10. What is a relationship and what are they?

Answer Database Relationship is defined as the connection

between the tables in a database. There are various data basing relationships, and they are as follows:

One to One Relationship.

One to Many Relationships.

Many to One Relationship.

Self-Referencing Relationship.

ORACLE SUPPORT INTERVIEW PART 3

Oracle support interview is a combination of Oracle Database related questions and SQL related questions. This is part of 5 Parts series and Third Part is shown below

Oracle related questions are given below:

Oracle (PL/SQL) Interview Questions

Question 1. What is a query?

Answer A DB query is a code written in order to get the information back from the database. Query can be designed in such a way that it matched with our expectation of the result set. Simply, a question to the Database.

Question 2. What is sub query?

Answer A sub query is a query within another query. The outer query is called as main query, and inner query is called sub query. Sub Query is always executed first, and the result of sub query is passed on to the main query.

Question 3. What are the types of sub query?

Answer There are two types of sub query – Correlated and Non-Correlated.A correlated sub query cannot be considered as independent query, but it can refer the column in a table listed in the FROM the list of the main query.

A Non-Correlated sub query can be considered as independent query and the output of sub query are substituted in the main query.

Question 4. What is a stored procedure?

Answer Stored Procedure is a function consists of many SQL statement to access the database system. Several SQL statements are consolidated into a stored procedure and execute them whenever and wherever required.

Oracle:

Sybase users

The Sybase stored procedure for this tutorial has five arguments, two of which have default values:

create procedure newPart @pno PartType, @desc varchar(40),

@price money

@quant int = 0, @reorder int = 10

as

The following code converts the part number to uppercase:

declare @newPno PartType

select @newPno = upper(@pno)

If the quantity and reorder quantity values are NULL, the default values are used:

if @quant is NULL

select @quant = 0

if @reorder is NULL

select @reorder = 10

The following coA   Q`de inserts the record into the Inventory table:

insert into Inventory (Part_Number, Description, Price,

Quantity_On_Hand, Reorder_Quantity)

values (@newPno,@desc,@price,@quant,@reorder)

We select the fields from the record that we just inserted and use them as the return value of the procedure. These values will be displayed in DBPak widgets.

select Part_Number, Description, Price, Quantity_On_Hand,

Reorder_Quantity from Inventory where

Part_Number = @newPno

This is the complete stored procedure. The next step is to use it in Database Xcessory. We will create a data entry screen with the Schema Browser

Question 5. What is a trigger?

Answer A DB trigger is a code or programs that automatically execute with response to some event on a table or view in a database. Mainly, trigger helps to maintain the integrity of the database.

Example: When a new student is added to the student database, new records should be created in the related tables like Exam, Score and Attendance tables.

Question 6.   What is the difference between DELETE and TRUNCATE commands?

Answer DELETE command is used to remove rows from the table, and WHERE clause can be used for conditional set of parameters. Commit and Rollback can be performed after delete statement.

TRUNCATE removes all rows from the table. Truncate operation cannot be rolled back.

Question 7.   What are local and global variables and their differences?

Answer Local variables are the variables which can be used or exist inside the function. They are not known to the other functions and those variables cannot be referred or used. Variables can be created whenever that function is called. Global variables are the variables which can be used or exist throughout the program. Same variable declared in global cannot be used in functions. Global variables cannot be created whenever that function is called.

Question 8. What is a constraint?

Answer Constraint can be used to specify the limit on the data type of table. Constraint can be specified while creating or altering the table statement. Sample of constraint are.

NOT NULL.

CHECK.

DEFAULT.

UNIQUE.

PRIMARY KEY.

FOREIGN KEY.

Question 9. What is data Integrity?

Answer Data Integrity defines the accuracy and consistency of data stored in a database. It can also define integrity constraints to enforce business rules on the data when it is entered into the application or database.

Question 10. What is Auto Increment?

Answer Auto increment keyword allows the user to create a unique number to be generated when a new record is inserted into the table. AUTO INCREMENT keyword can be used in Oracle and IDENTITY keyword can be used in SQL SERVER.

Mostly this keyword can be used whenever PRIMARY KEY is used.

ORACLE SUPPORT INTERVIEWS PART 4

Oracle support interview is a combination of Oracle Database related questions and SQL related questions. This is part of 5 Parts series and Fourth Part is shown below .Oracle related questions are given below:

Oracle (PL/SQL) Interview Questions

Question 1. What is the difference between Cluster and Non-Cluster Index?

Answer Clustered index is used for easy retrieval of data from the database by altering the way that the records are stored. Database sorts out rows by the column which is set to be clustered index.

A non clustered index does not alter the way it was stored but creates a complete separate object within the table. It point back to the original table rows after searching.

Question 2. What is Data warehouse?

Answer Data warehouse is a central repository of data from multiple sources of information. Those data are consolidated, transformed and made available for the mining and online processing. Warehouse data have a subset of data called Data Marts.

Question 3. What is Self-Join?

Answer Self-join is set to be query used to compare to itself. This is used to compare values in a column with other values in the same column in the same table. ALIAS ES can be used for the same table comparison.

Question 4. What is Cross-Join?

Answer Cross join defines as Cartesian product where number of rows in the first table multiplied by number of rows in the second table. If suppose, WHERE clause is used in cross join then the query will work like an INNER JOIN.

Question 5. What is user defined functions?

Answer User defined functions are the functions written to use that logic whenever required. It is not necessary to write the same logic several times. Instead, function can be called or executed whenever needed.

Question 6. What are all types of user defined functions?

Three types of user defined functions are.

• Scalar Functions.

• Inline Table valued functions.

• Multi statement valued functions.

Scalar returns unit, variant defined the return clause. Other two types return table as a return.

Question 7. What is collation?

Collation is defined as set of rules that determine how character data can be sorted and compared. This can be used to compare A and, other language characters and also depends on the width of the characters.

ASCII value can be used to compare these character data.

Question 8. What are all different types of collation sensitivity?

Following are different types of collation sensitivity -.

• Case Sensitivity – A and a and B and b.

• Accent Sensitivity.

• Kana Sensitivity – Japanese Kana characters.

• Width Sensitivity – Single byte character and double byte character.

Question 9. Advantages and Disadvantages of Stored Procedure?

Stored procedure can be used as a modular programming – means create once, store and call for several times whenever required. This supports faster execution instead of executing multiple queries. This reduces network traffic and provides better security to the data.

Disadvantage is that it can be executed only in the Database and utilizes more memory in the database server.

Question 10. What is Online Transaction Processing (OLTP)?

Online Transaction Processing or OLTP manages transaction based applications which can be used for data entry and easy retrieval processing of data. This processing makes like easier on simplicity and efficiency. It is faster, more accurate results and expenses with respect to OTLP.

Example – Bank Transactions on a daily basis.

Question 11. What is CLAUSE?

SQL clause is defined to limit the result set by providing condition to the query. This usually filters some rows from the whole set of records.

Example – Query that has WHERE condition

Query that has HAVING condition.

Question 12. What is recursive stored procedure?

A stored procedure which calls by itself until it reaches some boundary condition. This recursive function or procedure helps programmers to use the same set of code any number of times.

Question 13. What is Union, minus and Interact commands?

UNION operator is used to combine the results of two tables, and it eliminates duplicate rows from the tables.

MINUS operator is used to return rows from the first query but not from the second query. Matching records of first and second query and other rows from the first query will be displayed as a result set.

INTERSECT operator is used to return rows returned by both the queries.

Question 14. What is an ALIAS command?

ALIAS name can be given to a table or column. This alias name can be referred in WHERE clause to identify the table or column.

Question 15. What is the difference between TRUNCATE and DROP statements?

TRUNCATE removes all the rows from the table, and it cannot be rolled back. DROP command removes a table from the database and operation cannot be rolled back.

Question 16. What are the aggregate and scalar functions?

Aggregate functions are used to evaluate mathematical calculation and return single values. This can be calculated from the columns in a table. Scalar functions return a single value based on the input value.

Example -.

Aggregate – max(), count – Calculated with respect to numeric.

Scalar – UCASE(), NOW() – Calculated with respect to strings.

Question 17. How can you create an empty table from an existing table?

Example will be –

Select * into studentcopy from student where 1=2.

Here, we are copying student table to another table with the same structure with no rows copied.

Question 18. How to fetch alternate records from a table?

Records can be fetched for both Odd and Even row numbers -.

To display even numbers-.

1 Select studentId from (Select rowno, studentId from student) where mod(rowno,2)=0.

To display odd numbers-.

1 Select studentId from (Select rowno, studentId from student) where mod(rowno,2)=1.

Question 19. How to select unique records from a table?

Select unique records from a table by using DISTINCT keyword.

Select DISTINCT StudentID, StudentName from Student.

Question 20. What is the command used to fetch first 5 characters of the string?

There are many ways to fetch first 5 characters of the string -.

Select SUBSTRING(StudentName,1,5) as studentname from

student.

Select RIGHT(Studentname,5) as studentname from student.

ORACLE SUPPORT INTERVIEWS PART 5

Oracle support interview is a combination of Oracle Database related questions and SQL related questions. This is part of 5 Parts series and Final Part is shown below

Oracle related questions are given below:

Oracle (PL/SQL) Interview Questions

Question 1. Which operator is used in query for pattern matching?

LIKE operator is used for pattern matching, and it can be used as -.

1. % – Matches zero or more characters.

2. _(Underscore) – Matching exactly one character.

Question 2.What is join? explain inner,outer,self join

Answer Joins are used in queries to explain how different tables are related. Joins also let you select data from a table depending upon data from another table.

Types of joins: INNER JOINs, OUTER JOINs, CROSS JOINs. OUTER JOINs are further classified as LEFT OUTER JOINS, RIGHT OUTER JOINS and FULL OUTER JOINS.

Self join is just like any other join, except that two instances of the same table will be joined in the query.

Question 3. difference between truncate delete drop

Answer: Dropping : (Table structure + Data are deleted), Invalidates the dependent objects ,Drops the indexes

Truncating: (Data alone deleted), Performs an automatic commit, Faster than delete

Delete : (Data alone deleted), Doesn't perform automatic commit

Question 4. What is cursor,ref cursor,cursor for loop?

Answer: Cursors allow row-by-row processing of the result sets.

Types of cursors: Static, Dynamic, Forward-only, Keyset-driven. See books online for more information.

Disadvantages of cursors: Each time you fetch a row from the cursor, it results in a network roundtrip, whereas a normal SELECT query makes only one rowundtrip, however large the resultset is. Cursors are also costly because they require more resources and temporary storage (results in more IO operations). Furthere, there are restrictions on the

SELECT statements that can be used with some types of cursors.

Cursors are used by database programmers to process individual rows returned by database system queries . A cursor can be viewed as a pointer to one row in a set of rows.

To use cursors in SQL procedures, you need to do the following:

1. Declare a cursor that defines a result set.

DECLARE cursor_name CURSOR FOR SELECT ... FROM ...

2. Open the cursor to establish the result set.

OPEN cursor_name

3. Fetch the data into local variables as needed from the cursor,

one row at a time.

FETCH cursor_name INTO ...

4. Close the cursor when done.

CLOSE cursor_name

There are two types of cursors in PL/SQL:

Implicit cursors:These are created by default when DML statements like, INSERT, UPDATE, and DELETE statements are executed. They are also created when a SELECT statement that returns just one row is executed.

Explicit cursors:They must be created when you are executing a SELECT statement that returns more than one row. Even though the cursor stores multiple records, only one record can be processed at a time, which is called as current row. When you fetch a row the current row position moves to next row.

Both implicit and explicit cursors have the same functionality, but they differ in the way they are accessed.

Implicit Cursors: Application

When you execute DML statements like DELETE, INSERT, UPDATE and SELECT statements, implicit statements are created to process these statements.

Oracle provides few attributes called as implicit cursor attributes to check the status of DML operations. The cursor attributes available are %FOUND, %NOTFOUND, %ROWCOUNT, and %ISOPEN.

For example, When you execute INSERT, UPDATE, or DELETE statements the cursor attributes tell us whether any rows are affected and how many have been affected.

When a SELECT... INTO statement is executed in a PL/SQL Block, implicit cursor attributes can be used to find out whether any row has been returned by the SELECT statement. PL/SQL returns an error when no data is selected.

The status of the cursor for each of these attributes are defined in the below table.

Attributes Return Value Example

%FOUND The return value is TRUE, if the DML statements like INSERT, DELETE and UPDATE affect at least one row and if SELECT ....INTO statement return at least one row. SQL%FOUND

The return value is FALSE, if DML statements like INSERT, DELETE and UPDATE do not affect row and if SELECT....INTO statement do not return a row.

%NOTFOUND The return value is FALSE, if DML statements like INSERT, DELETE and UPDATE at least one row and if SELECT ....INTO statement return at least one row. SQL%NOTFOUND

The return value is TRUE, if a DML statement like INSERT, DELETE and UPDATE do not affect even one row and if SELECT ....INTO statement does not return a row.

%ROWCOUNT Return the number of rows affected by the DML operations INSERT, DELETE, UPDATE, SELECT SQL%ROWCOUNT

For Example: Consider the PL/SQL Block that uses implicit cursor attributes as shown below:

```
DECLARE var_rows number(5);
BEGIN
UPDATE employee
SET salary = salary + 1000;
IF SQL%NOTFOUND THEN
dbms_output.put_line('None of the salaries where updated');
ELSIF SQL%FOUND THEN
```

```
var_rows := SQL%ROWCOUNT;

dbms_output.put_line('Salaries for ' || var_rows || 'employees are updated');

END IF;

END;
```

In the above PL/SQL Block, the salaries of all the employees in the 'employee' table are updated. If none of the employee's salary are updated we get a message 'None of the salaries where updated'. Else we get a message like for example, 'Salaries for 1000 employees are updated' if there are 1000 rows in 'employee' table.

A REF CURSOR is basically a data type. A variable created based on such a data type is generally called a cursor variable. A cursor variable can be associated with different queries at run-time. The primary advantage of using cursor variables is their capability to pass result sets between sub programs (like stored procedures, functions, packages etc.).

Let us start with a small sub-program as follows:

```
declare

type r_cursor is REF CURSOR;

c_emp r_cursor;

en emp.ename%type;

begin

open c_emp for select ename from emp;

loop

fetch c_emp into en;

exit when c_emp%notfound;

dbms_output.put_line(en);

end loop;

close c_emp;
```

end;

Let me explain step by step. The following is the first statement you need to understand:

type r_cursor is REF CURSOR;

The above statement simply defines a new data type called "r_cursor," which is of the type REF CURSOR. We declare a cursor variable named "c_emp" based on the type "r_cursor" as follows:

c_emp r_cursor;

Every cursor variable must be opened with an associated SELECT statement as follows:

open c_emp for select ename from emp;

To retrieve each row of information from the cursor, I used a loop together with a FETCH statement as follows:

loop

fetch c_emp into en;

exit when c_emp%notfound;

dbms_output.put_line(en);

end loop;

I finally closed the cursor using the following statement:

close c_emp;

%ROWTYPE with REF CURSOR

In the previous section, I retrieved only one column (ename) of information using REF CURSOR. Now I would like to retrieve more than one column (or entire row) of information using the same. Let us consider the following example:

declare

type r_cursor is REF CURSOR;

c_emp r_cursor;

er emp%rowtype;

begin

open c_emp for select * from emp;

loop

fetch c_emp into er;

exit when c_emp%notfound;

dbms_output.put_line(er.ename || ' – ' || er.sal);

end loop;

close c_emp;

end;

In the above example, the only crucial declaration is the following:

er emp%rowtype;

The above declares a variable named "er," which can hold an entire row from the "emp" table. To retrieve the values (of each column) from that variable, we use the dot notation as follows:

dbms_output.put_line(er.ename || ' – ' || er.sal);

Question 6. What the difference between function and procedure is

Answer:

Top of Form

• Procedure can return zero or n values whereas function can return one value which is mandatory.

• Procedures can have input/output parameters for it whereas functions can have only input parameters.

• Procedure allows select as well as DML statement in it whereas function allows only select statement in it.

• Functions can be called from procedure whereas procedures cannot be called from function.

• Exception can be handled by try-catch block in a procedure whereas try-catch block cannot be used in a function.

• We can go for transaction management in procedure whereas we can't go in function.

• Procedures can not be utilized in a select statement whereas function can be embedded in a select statement.

• UDF can be used in the SQL statements anywhere in the WHERE/HAVING/SELECT section where as Stored procedures cannot be.

• UDFs that return tables can be treated as another rowset. This can be used in JOINs with other tables.

• Inline UDF's can be though of as views that take parameters and can be used in JOINs and other Rowsetoperations

Question 7.what is SQL LOADER how it works to load data from flat file to table

SQL*Loader is a tool used by DBAs and developers to populate Oracle tables with data from flat files. The SQL*Loader gives a lot of flexibility to selectively load certain columns but not others, or to exclude certain records entirely. SQL*Loader has some advantages over programming languages that allow embedded SQL statements, as well. SQL*Loader consist of understanding its elements. The first is the data to be loaded, which is stored in the datafile (this is basically a flat/text file, and should not be confused with Oracle Server datafiles, that make up the database). The second is the control file (this is basically a text file, acting as a directive to the Loader, it should not be confused with Oracle Servers control file, which holds database-related information). SQL*Loader accepts special parameters that can affect how the load occurs, called command-line parameters. These parameters which include the ID (username/password or commonly know as the schema) to use while loading data, the name of the data file, and the name of the control file.

SQL*Loader in action consist of several additional items. If, in the course of performing data loads, SQL*Loader encounters records it cannot load, the record is rejected and the SQL*Loader puts it in special file called bad file. Additionally, SQL*Loader gives the user options to reject data based on special criteria. These criteria are defined in the control file as a part of the when clause. Is the SQL*Loader encounters a record that fails a specified when clause, the record is placed in a special file called discard file.

Question 7.what is INSTR AND SUBSTR function

Substr

It allows you to extract a portion or subset of contiguous (connected) characters from a string. There are three arguments to it. In first argument the character string is given. In the second argument there the starting position id given from where the extraction should be started and in the third argument you provide the number of characters to be extracted.

SQL> select substr('Oracle',3,3) from dual;

SUB

—

acl

The INSTR function searches a string to find a match for the substring and, if found, returns the position, in the source string, of the first character of that substring. If there is no match, then INSTR returns 0.

First argument is a string, second argument is a string too, functions finds the string given in the second arguent from the string given in the first argument. Third and fourth arguments are optional, in third argument we tell the function from what position of the string in the 1st argument search should start. Say the string in 2nd argument appears two or three times in the string in the 1st argument then the fourth argument tells which appearance to find.

SQL> select instr('Oracle Corporation','r',1,3) INSTR

2 from dual;

INSTR

Question 8 : what is the difference between IN and Exists?

using the IN clause, you're telling the rule-based

optimizer that you want the inner query to drive the outer

query (think: IN = inside to outside).

When you write EXISTS in a where clause, you're telling the

optimizer that you want the outer query to be run first,

using each value to fetch a value from the inner query

(think: EXISTS = outside to inside).

Question 9 .what is index, how many types of index you know

An index is a performance-tuning method of allowing faster retrieval of records. An index creates an entry for each value that appears in the indexed columns. By default, Oracle creates B-tree indexes.

Question 10.what is trigger?

Oracle lets you define procedures called triggers that run implicitly when an INSERT, UPDATE, or DELETE statement is issued against the associated table or, in some cases, against a view, or when database system actions occur. These procedures can be written in PL/SQL or Java and stored in the database, or they can be written as C callouts.

Triggers are similar to stored procedures.

Question 11.what is database links?

Database Links The central concept in distributed database systems is a database link. A database link is a connection between two physical database servers that allows a client to access them as one logical database.

Question 12. what is the packages?

A package is a schema object that groups logically related PL/SQL types, items, and subprograms. Packages usually have two parts, a specification and a body, although sometimes the body is unnecessary. The specification (spec for short) is the interface to your applications; it declares the types, variables, constants, exceptions, cursors, and subprograms available for use. The body fully defines cursors and subprograms, and so implements the spec.

Question 13.what is diff between %notfound and no data found

NO DATA FOUND is an Exception whereas NOTFOUND is a cursor attribute

NO DATA FOUND: Is an exception which is raised when no rows are retrieved from the database in a SELECT statement

then PL/SQL raises the exception NO_DATA_FOUND.

SQL INTERVIEW QUESTIONS

What is SQL?

Answer: SQL stands for Structured Query Language, and it is used to communicate with the Database. This is a standard language used to perform tasks such as retrieval, updation, insertion, and deletion of data from a database.

The SQL language is subdivided into several language elements, including:

Clauses, which are constituent components of statements and queries.

Expressions, which can produce either scalar values, or tables consisting of columns and rows of data.

Predicates, which specify conditions that can be evaluated to SQL three-valued logic (3VL) or Boolean(true/false/unknown) truth values and which are used to limit the effects of statements and queries, or to change program flow.

Queries, which retrieve the data based on specific criteria. This is the most important element of SQL.

Statements, which may have a persistent effect on schemata and data, or which may control transactions, program flow, connections, sessions, or diagnostics.

Queries: The most common operation in SQL is the query, which is performed with the declarative SELECT statement. SELECT retrieves data from one or more tables, or expressions.

A query includes a list of columns to be included in the final result immediately following the SELECT keyword. An asterisk ("*") can also be used to specify that the query should return all columns of the queried tables. SELECT is the most complex statement in SQL, with optional keywords and clauses that include:

The FROM clause which indicates the table(s) from which data is to be retrieved. The FROM clause can include optional JOIN subclauses to specify the rules for joining tables.

The WHERE clause includes a comparison predicate, which restricts the rows returned by the query. The WHERE clause eliminates all rows from the result set for which the comparison predicate does not evaluate to True.

The GROUP BY clause is used to project rows having common values into a smaller set of rows. GROUP BY is often used in conjunction with SQL aggregation functions or to eliminate duplicate rows from a result set. The WHERE clause is applied before the GROUP BY clause.

The HAVING clause includes a predicate used to filter rows resulting from the GROUP BY clause. Because it acts on the results of the GROUP BY clause, aggregation functions can be used in the HAVING clause predicate.

The ORDER BY clause identifies which columns are used to sort the resulting data, and in which direction they should be sorted (options are ascending or descending). Without an ORDER BY clause, the order of rows returned by an SQL query is undefined.

SQL combines the roles of data definition, data manipulation, and query in a single language. It was one of the first commercial languages for the relational model, although it departs in some respects from the relational model as described by Codd (for example, the rows and columns of a table can be ordered).

Question 1: What are DBMS and RDBMS?

Answer: Database: A database is an organized collection of data.

DBMS: A Database Management System (DBMS) is a program that controls the creation, maintenance, and use of a database. DBMS can be termed as a File Manager that manages data in a database rather than saving it in file systems.

The interactions catered for by most existing DBMS fall into four main groups:

Data definition. Defining new data structures for a database, removing data structures from the database, modifying the structure of existing data.

Update. Inserting, modifying, and deleting data.

Retrieval. Obtaining information either for end-user queries and reports or for processing by applications.

Administration. Registering and monitoring users, enforcing data security, monitoring performance, maintaining data integrity, dealing with concurrency control, and recovering information if the system fails.

A DBMS is responsible for maintaining the integrity and security of stored data, and for recovering information if the system fails.

Benefits of DBMS:

Reduce data redundancy.

Reduce data inconsistencies.

Multiple Access.

Data Integrity (Data accuracy).

Data Security.

RDBMS stands for Relational Database Management System. RDBMS stores the data into the collection of tables, which is related by common fields between the columns of the table. It also provides relational operators to manipulate the data stored in the tables.

A relational database management system (RDBMS) is a database management system (DBMS) that is based on the relational model as introduced by E. F. Codd,

Rule 000: A RDBMS system should be capable of using its relational facilities (exclusively) to manage the database.

Rule 1: The information rule: All information in the database is to be represented in one and only one way. This is achieved by values in column positions within rows of tables.

Rule 2: The guaranteed access rule: All data must be accessible with no ambiguity. This is achieved in the RDBMS by using the primary key concept.

Rule 3: Systematic treatment of null values: The DBMS must allow each field to remain null. The null can be stored in any field of any data type.

Rule 4: Active online catalog based on the relational model:

The authorized users can access the database structure by using common language i.e SQL.

Rule 5: The comprehensive data sublanguage rule: The system must support at least one relational language that has simple syntax and transaction management facilities. It can be used in the application as well as in the RDBMS systems.

Rule 6: The view updating rule: All views must be updatable by the system.

Rule 7: High-level insert, update, and delete: The system can insert, update, and delete operations fully. It can also perform the operations on multiple rows simultaneously.

Rule 8: Physical data independence: Changes to the physical storage structure must not require a change to an application based on the structure.

Rule 9: Logical data independence: Changes to the logical level (tables, columns, rows, and so on) must not require a change to an application based on the structure.

Rule 10: Integrity independence: All the Integrity constraints like primary key, uniques key, etc must be specified separately from application programs and stored in the catalog.

Rule 11: Distribution independence: The distribution of portions of the database to various locations should be invisible to users of the database.

Rule 12: The nonsubversion rule: If the system provides a low-level (record-at-a-time) interface, then that interface cannot be used to subvert the system, for example, bypassing a relational security or integrity constraint.

Question 3: What are the components of SQL?

Answer: Data Definition Language (DDL): It's a set of SQL commands used to create modify and delete database structures but not the data.DDL manages table and index structure. The most basic items of DDL are CREATE, ALTER, RENAME, DROP and TRUNCATE statements:

CREATE creates an object (a table, for example) in the database, e.g.:

CREATE TABLE My_table(my_field1 INT, my_field2 VARCHAR(50), my_field3 DATE NOT NULL, PRIMARY KEY (my_field1, my_field2));

ALTER modifies the structure of an existing object in various ways, for example, adding a column to an existing table or a constraint, e.g.:

ALTER TABLE My_table ADD my_field4 NUMBER(3) NOT NULL;

TRUNCATE deletes all data from a table in a very fast way, deleting the data inside the table and not the table itself. It usually implies a subsequent COMMIT operation, i.e., it cannot be rolled back (data is not written to the logs for rollback later, unlike DELETE).

TRUNCATE TABLE My_table;

DROP deletes an object in the database, usually irretrievably, i.e., it cannot be rolled back, e.g.:

DROP TABLE My_table;

Data manipulation The Data Manipulation Language (DML) is the subset of SQL used to add, update and delete data:

INSERT adds rows (formally tuples) to an existing table, e.g.:

INSERT INTO My_table (field1, field2, field3)

VALUES ('test', 'N', NULL);

UPDATE modifies a set of existing table rows, e.g.:

UPDATE My_table SET field1 = 'updated value' WHERE field2 = 'N';

DELETE removes existing rows from a table, e.g.:

DELETE FROM My_table WHERE field2 = 'N';

MERGE is used to combine the data of multiple tables. It combines the INSERT and UPDATE elements.

MERGE INTO TABLE_NAME USING table_reference ON (condition)

WHEN MATCHED THEN

UPDATE SET column1 = value1 [, column2 = value2 ...]

WHEN NOT MATCHED THEN

INSERT (column1 [, column2 ...]) VALUES (value1 [, value2 ...])

Transaction controls: It is component of SQL statement that control access to data. Transactions, if available, wrap DML operations:

START TRANSACTION (or BEGIN WORK, or BEGIN TRANSACTION, depending on SQL dialect) marks the start of a database transaction, which either completes entirely or not at all.

SAVE TRANSACTION (or SAVEPOINT) saves the state of the database at the current point in transaction

CREATE TABLE tbl_1(id INT);

INSERT INTO tbl_1(id) VALUES(1);

INSERT INTO tbl_1(id) VALUES(2);

COMMIT;

UPDATE tbl_1 SET id=200 WHERE id=1;

SAVEPOINT id_1upd;

UPDATE tbl_1 SET id=1000 WHERE id=2;

ROLLBACK TO id_1upd;

SELECT id FROM tbl_1;

COMMIT causes all data changes in a transaction to be made permanent.

ROLLBACK causes all data changes since the last COMMIT or ROLLBACK to be discarded, leaving the state of the data as it was prior to those changes.

Once the COMMIT statement completes, the transaction's changes cannot be rolled back.

COMMIT and ROLLBACK terminate the current transaction and release data locks. In the absence of a START TRANSACTION or similar statement, the semantics of SQL are implementation-dependent. The following example shows a classic transfer of funds transaction, where money is removed from one account and added to another. If either the removal or the addition fails, the entire transaction is rolled back.

START TRANSACTION;

UPDATE Account SET amount=amount-200 WHERE account_number=1234;

UPDATE Account SET amount=amount+200 WHERE account_number=2345;

IF ERRORS=0 COMMIT;

IF ERRORS<>0 ROLLBACK;

Question 4: What is Normalization and why it is used? What is Denormalization?

Answer: In the design of a relational database management system (RDBMS), the process of organizing data to minimize redundancy is called normalization.

The goal of database normalization is to decompose relations with anomalies in order to produce smaller, well-structured relations. Normalization usually involves dividing large tables into smaller (and less redundant) tables and defining relationships between them. The objective is to isolate data so that additions, deletions, and modifications of a field can be made in just one table and then propagated through the rest of the database via the defined relationships.

Normalization is the process of minimizing redundancy and

dependency by organizing fields and table of a database. The main aim of Normalization is to add, delete or modify field that can be made in a single table.

De Normalization is a technique used to access the data from higher to lower normal forms of the database. It is also a process of introducing redundancy into a table by incorporating data from the related tables.

First Normal Form (1NF):.This should remove all the duplicate columns from the table. Creation of tables for the related data and identification of unique columns.

Second Normal Form (2NF): Meeting all requirements of the first normal form. Placing the subsets of data in separate tables and Creation of relationships between the tables using primary keys.

Third Normal Form (3NF): This should meet all requirements of 2NF. Removing the columns which are not dependent on primary key constraints.

Fourth Normal Form (3NF): Meeting all the requirements of third normal form and it should not have multi- valued dependencies.

Question 5: What is the primary key? What is a unique key? What is a foreign key?

Answer: A primary key is a combination of fields that uniquely specify a row. This is a special kind of unique key, and it has an implicit NOT NULL constraint. It means Primary key values cannot be NULL.

A Unique key constraint uniquely identified each record in the database. This provides uniqueness for the column or set of columns. A Primary key constraint has an automatic unique constraint defined on it. But not, in the case of Unique Key. There can be many unique constraints defined per table, but only one Primary key constraint defined per table.

Question:

a foreign key is one table that can be related to the primary key of another table. The relationship needs to be created between two tables by referencing foreign keys with the primary key of another table.

Question 6: What is an Index?

Answer An index is a performance tuning method of allowing faster retrieval of records from the table. An index creates an entry for each value and it will be faster to retrieve data.

Unique Index. This indexing does not allow the field to have duplicate values if the column is unique indexed. A unique index can be applied automatically when the primary key is defined.

Clustered Index. This type of index reorders the physical order of the table and search based on the key values. Each table can have only one clustered index. A clustered index is used for easy retrieval of data from the database by altering the way that the records are stored. Database sorts out rows by the column which is set to be clustered index.

Non-Clustered Index. Non-Clustered Index does not alter the physical order of the table and maintains the logical order of data. Each table can have 999 non clustered indexes. A non clustered index does not alter the way it was stored but creates a completely separate object within the table. It points back to the original table rows after searching.

Question 7: What is a join?

Answer: This is a keyword used to query data from more tables based on the relationship between the fields of the tables. Keys play a major role when JOINs are used.

There are various types of join that can be used to retrieve data and it depends on the relationship between tables.

Inner join.Inner join return rows when there is at least one match of rows between the tables.

Right Join.Right join return rows which are common between the tables and all rows of Right hand side table. Simply, it returns all the rows from the right hand side table even though there are no matches in the left hand side table.

Left Join.Left join return rows which are common between the tables and all rows of Left hand side table. Simply, it returns all the rows from Left hand side table even though there are no matches in the Right hand side table.

Full Join.Full join return rows when there are matching rows in any one of the tables. This means, it returns all the rows from the left hand side table and all the rows from the right hand side table.

Self-join is set to be query used to compare to itself. This is used to compare values in a column with other values in the same column in the same table. ALIAS ES can be used for the same table comparison.

Cross join defines as Cartesian product where number of rows in the first table multiplied by the number of rows in the second table. If suppose, WHERE clause is used in cross join then the query will work like an INNER JOIN.

Question 8: What is a View?

Answer A view is a virtual table that consists of a subset of data contained in a table. Views are not virtually present, and it takes less space to store. View can have data of one or more tables combined, and it is depending on the relationship.

Question 9. What is a Cursor?

Answer A database Cursor is a control that enables traversal over the rows or records in the table. This can be viewed as a pointer to one row in a set of rows. The cursor is very much useful for traversing such as retrieval, addition, and removal of database records.

Cursors allow row-by-row processing of the resultsets.

Types of cursors: Static, Dynamic, Forward-only, Keyset-driven. See books online for more information.

Disadvantages of cursors: Each time you fetch a row from the cursor, it results in a network roundtrip, where as a normal SELECT query makes only one rowundtrip, however large the resultset is. Cursors are also costly because they require more resources and temporary storage (results in more IO operations). Furthere, there are restrictions on the SELECT statements that can be used with some types of cursors.

Cursors are used by database programmers to process individual rows returned by database system queries . A cursor can be viewed as a pointer to one row in a set of rows.

To use cursors in SQL procedures, you need to do the following:

1. Declare a cursor that defines a result set.

DECLARE cursor_name CURSOR FOR SELECT ... FROM ...

2. Open the cursor to establish the result set.

OPEN cursor_name

3. Fetch the data into local variables as needed from the cursor, one row at a time.

FETCH cursor_name INTO ...

4. Close the cursor when done.

CLOSE cursor_name

PL/SQL —à ORACLE

There are two types of cursors in PL/SQL:

Implicit cursors: These are created by default when DML statements like, INSERT, UPDATE, and DELETE statements are executed. They are also created when a SELECT statement that returns just one row is executed.

Explicit cursors: They must be created when you are executing a SELECT statement that returns more than one row. Even though the cursor stores multiple records, only one record can be processed at a time, which is called a current row. When you fetch a row the current row position moves to the next row.

Both implicit and explicit cursors have the same functionality, but they differ in the way they are accessed.

Implicit Cursors: Application

When you execute DML statements like DELETE, INSERT, UPDATE and SELECT statements, implicit statements are created to process these statements.

Oracle provides few attributes called as implicit cursor attributes to check the status of DML operations. The cursor attributes available are %FOUND, %NOTFOUND, %ROWCOUNT, and %ISOPEN.

For example, When you execute INSERT, UPDATE, or DELETE statements the cursor attributes tell us whether any rows are affected and how many have been affected.

When a SELECT... INTO statement is executed in a PL/SQL Block, implicit cursor attributes can be used to find out whether any row has been returned by the SELECT statement. PL/SQL returns an error when no data is selected.

The status of the cursor for each of these attributes is defined in the below table.

Attributes

Return Value

Example

%FOUND

The return value is TRUE, if the DML statements like INSERT,

DELETE and UPDATE affect at least one row and if SELECT ....INTO statement return at least one row.

SQL%FOUND

The return value is FALSE, if DML statements like INSERT, DELETE and UPDATE do not affect row and if SELECT....INTO statement do not return a row.

%NOTFOUND

The return value is FALSE, if DML statements like INSERT, DELETE and UPDATE at least one row and if SELECT ....INTO statement return at least one row.

SQL%NOTFOUND

The return value is TRUE, if a DML statement like INSERT, DELETE and UPDATE do not affect even one row and if SELECT ....INTO statement does not return a row.

%ROWCOUNT

Return the number of rows affected by the DML operations INSERT, DELETE, UPDATE, SELECT

SQL%ROWCOUNT

For Example: Consider the PL/SQL Block that uses implicit cursor attributes as shown below:

```
DECLARE var_rows number(5);
```

```
BEGIN

UPDATE employee

SET salary = salary + 1000;

IF SQL%NOTFOUND THEN

dbms_output.put_line('None of the salaries where updated');

ELSIF SQL%FOUND THEN

var_rows := SQL%ROWCOUNT;

dbms_output.put_line('Salaries for ' || var_rows || 'employees are
updated');

END IF;

END;
```

In the above PL/SQL Block, the salaries of all the employees in the 'employee' table are updated. If none of the employee's salary are updated we get a message 'None of the salaries where updated'. Else we get a message like for example, 'Salaries for 1000 employees are updated' if there are 1000 rows in 'employee' table.

A REF CURSOR is basically a data type. A variable created based on such a data type is generally called a cursor variable. A cursor variable can be associated with different queries at run-time. The primary advantage of using cursor variables is their capability to pass result sets between sub programs (like stored procedures, functions, packages etc.).

Let us start with a small sub-program as follows:

```
declare
type r_cursor is REF CURSOR;
c_emp r_cursor;
en emp.ename%type;
begin
open c_emp for select ename from emp;
loop
fetch c_emp into en;
exit when c_emp%notfound;
dbms_output.put_line(en);
end loop;
close c_emp;
end;
```

Let me explain step by step. The following is the first statement you need to understand:

```
type r_cursor is REF CURSOR;
```

The above statement simply defines a new data type called "r_cursor," which is of the type REF CURSOR. We declare a cursor variable named "c_emp" based on the type "r_cursor" as follows:

```
c_emp r_cursor;
```

Every cursor variable must be opened with an associated SELECT statement as follows:

```
open c_emp for select ename from emp;
```

To retrieve each row of information from the cursor, I used a loop together with a FETCH statement as follows:

```
loop
fetch c_emp into en;
exit when c_emp%notfound;
dbms_output.put_line(en);
end loop;
```

I finally closed the cursor using the following statement:

```
close c_emp;
```

%ROWTYPE with REF CURSOR

In the previous section, I retrieved only one column (ename) of information using REF CURSOR. Now I would like to retrieve more than one column (or entire row) of information using the same. Let us consider the following example:

```
declare
type r_cursor is REF CURSOR;
c_emp r_cursor;
er emp%rowtype;
begin
open c_emp for select * from emp;
```

loop

fetch c_emp into er;

exit when c_emp%notfound;

dbms_output.put_line(er.ename || ' – ' || er.sal);

end loop;

close c_emp;

end;

In the above example, the only crucial declaration is the following:

er emp%rowtype;

The above declares a variable named "er," which can hold an entire row from the "emp" table. To retrieve the values (of each column) from that variable, we use the dot notation as follows:

dbms_output.put_line(er.ename || ' – ' || er.sal);

Question 10. What is the relationship and what are they?

Answer Database Relationship is defined as the connection between the tables in a database. There are various data base relationships, and they are as follows:.

One to One Relationship.

One to Many Relationship.

Many to One Relationship.

Self-Referencing Relationship.

Question 11. What is a query? What is subquery?

Answer A DB query is a code written in order to get the

information back from the database. Query can be designed in such a way that it matched with our expectation of the result set. Simply, a question to the Database.

A subquery is a query within another query. The outer query is called as main query, and inner query is called subquery. SubQuery is always executed first, and the result of subquery is passed on to the main query.

There are two types of subquery – Correlated and Non-Correlated.

A correlated subquery cannot be considered as an independent query, but it can refer the column in a table listed in the FROM the list of the main query.

A Non-Correlated sub query can be considered as an independent query and the output of subquery are substituted in the main query.

Question 12. What is a stored procedure?

Answer Stored Procedure is a function that consists of many SQL statements to access the database system. Several SQL statements are consolidated into a stored procedure and execute them whenever and wherever required.

Oracle:

Sybase users

The Sybase stored procedure for this tutorial has five arguments, two of which have default values:

create procedure newPart @pno PartType, @desc varchar(40),

```
@price money

@quant int = 0, @reorder int = 10

as
```

The following code converts the part number to uppercase:

```
declare @newPno PartType

select @newPno = upper(@pno)
```

If the quantity and reorder quantity values are NULL, the default values are used:

```
if @quant is NULL

select @quant = 0

if @reorder is NULL

select @reorder = 10
```

The following coA Q`de inserts the record into the Inventory table:

```
insert into Inventory (Part_Number, Description, Price,

Quantity_On_Hand, Reorder_Quantity)

values (@newPno,@desc,@price,@quant,@reorder )
```

We select the fields from the record that we just inserted and use them as the return value of the procedure. These values will be displayed in DBPak widgets.

select Part_Number, Description, Price, Quantity_On_Hand,

Reorder_Quantity from Inventory where

Part_Number = @newPno

This is the complete stored procedure. The next step is to use it in Database Xcessory. We will create a data entry screen with the Schema Browser.

Oracle users

The Oracle stored procedure for this tutorial has five arguments:

create or replace procedure newPart(

pno IN OUT char,

thePrice IN OUT NUMBER,

part_description IN varchar,

quantity_on_hand IN OUT integer,

reorder IN OUT integer

)

```
as

newPno CHAR(8);

quan integer := 0;

BEGIN
```

The following code converts the part number to uppercase:

```
newPno := UPPER(pno);
```

If the quantity and reorder quantity values are NULL, the default values are used:

```
IF (quantity_on_hand is not NULL) then

quan := quantity_on_hand;

end if;

IF (reorder is NULL) then

reorder := 10;

end if;
```

The following code inserts the record into the Inventory table:

```
INSERT INTO INVENTORY (PART_NUMBER, DESCRIPTION, PRICE,
```

QUANTITY_ON_HAND, REORDER_QUANTITY)

VALUES (newPno, part_description, thePrice, quan, reorder);

We select the fields from the record that we just inserted and store the values in the in/out parameters of the stored procedure. These values will be displayed in DBPak widgets.

SELECT   PART_NUMBER,   PRICE, QUANTITY_ON_HAND,REORDER_QUANTITY

INTO pno, thePrice, quantity_on_hand, reorder

FROM INVENTORY WHERE PART_NUMBER = newPno;

END

Stored procedure can be used as modular programming – means create once, store, and call for several times whenever required. This supports faster execution instead of executing multiple queries. This reduces network traffic and provides better security to the data.

The disadvantage is that it can be executed only in the Database and utilizes more memory in the database server.

What is a recursive stored procedure?

Answer A stored procedure that calls by itself until it reaches some boundary condition. This recursive function or procedure helps programmers to use the same set of code any number of times.

Question 13. What is a trigger?

Answer A DB trigger is a code or program that automatically execute with the response to some event on a table or view in a database. Mainly, the trigger helps to maintain the integrity of the database.

Example: When a new student is added to the student database, new records should be created in the related tables like Exam, Score, and Attendance tables.

Question 14. What is the difference between DELETE and TRUNCATE commands?

Answer: DELETE command is used to remove rows from the table, and the WHERE clause can be used for a conditional set of parameters. Commit and Rollback can be performed after the delete statement.

TRUNCATE removes all rows from the table. The truncate operation cannot be rolled back.

Question 15. What are local and global variables and their differences?

Answer Local variables are the variables that can be used or exist inside the function. They are not known to the other functions and those variables cannot be referred or used. Variables can be created whenever that function is called. Global variables are the variables that can be used or exist throughout the program. The same variable declared in global cannot be used in functions. Global variables cannot be created whenever that function is called.

Question 16. What is a constraint?

Answer Constraint can be used to specify the limit on the data type of table. The constraint can be specified while creating or altering the table statement. Sample of constraints are.

NOT NULL.

CHECK.

DEFAULT.

UNIQUE.

PRIMARY KEY.

FOREIGN KEY.

Question 17. What is Data Integrity?

Answer Data Integrity defines the accuracy and consistency of data stored in a database. It can also define integrity constraints to enforce business rules on the data when it is entered into the application or database.

Question 18. What is Auto Increment?

Answer Auto increment keyword allows the user to create a unique number to be generated when a new record is inserted into the table. AUTO INCREMENT keyword can be used in Oracle and IDENTITY keyword can be used in SQL SERVER.

Mostly this keyword can be used whenever PRIMARY KEY is used.

Question 19. What is Datawarehouse?

Answer Datawarehouse is a central repository of data from multiple sources of information. Those data are consolidated, transformed and made available for the mining and online processing. Warehouse data have a subset of data called Data Marts.

Question 20. What are user-defined functions? What are all types of user defined functions?

Answer User-defined functions are the functions written to use that logic whenever required. It is not necessary to write the same logic several times. Instead, the function can be called or executed whenever needed.

Three types of user-defined functions are.

Scalar Functions.

Inline Table valued functions.

Multi statement valued functions.

Scalar returns unit, variant defined the return clause. Other two types return table as a return.

Question 21. What is CLAUSE?

Answer SQL clause is defined to limit the result set by providing conditions to the query. This usually filters some rows from the whole set of records.

Example – Query that has WHERE condition

A query that has HAVING condition.

Question 23. What is an ALIAS command?

Answer ALIAS name can be given to a table or column. This alias name can be referred in WHERE clause to identify the table or column.

Question 24. What is the difference between TRUNCATE and DROP statements?

Answer TRUNCATE removes all the rows from the table, and it cannot be rolled back. DROP command removes a table from the database and operation cannot be rolled back.

Question 25. What are the aggregate and scalar functions?

Answer Aggregate functions are used to evaluate mathematical calculations and return single values. This can be calculated from the columns in a table. Scalar functions return a single value based on the input value.

Example -.

Aggregate – max(), count – Calculated with respect to numeric.

Scalar – UCASE(), NOW() – Calculated with respect to strings.

Question 26. How can you create an empty table from an existing table?

Answer An example will be -.

Select * into studentcopy from student where 1=2.

Here, we are copying student table to another table with the same structure with no rows copied.

Question 27. How to fetch alternate records from a table?

Answer Records can be fetched for both Odd and Even row numbers -.

To display even numbers-.

Select studentId from (Select rowno, studentId from student) where mod(rowno,2)=0.

To display odd numbers-.

Select studentId from (Select rowno, studentId from student) where mod(rowno,2)=1.

Question 28. How to select unique records from a table?

Answer Select unique records from a table by using DISTINCT keyword.

Select DISTINCT StudentID, StudentName from Student.

Question 29. What is the command used to fetch first 5 characters of the string?

Answer There are many ways to fetch first 5 characters of the string -.

Select SUBSTRING(StudentName,1,5) as studentname from student.

Select RIGHT(Studentname,5) as studentname from student.

Question 30. Which operator is used in query for pattern matching?

LIKE operator is used for pattern matching, and it can be used as -.

% – Matches zero or more characters.

_(Underscore) – Matching exactly one character.

Select * from Student where studentname like 'a%'

Select * from Student where studentname like 'ami_'

Question 31. What is Union, minus and Interact commands?

Answer: UNION operator is used to combining the results of two tables, and it eliminates duplicate rows from the tables.

MINUS operator is used to return rows from the first query but not from the second query. Matching records of first and second query and other rows from the first query will be displayed as a result set.

INTERSECT operator is used to return rows returned by both the queries.

Question 32 .what is the difference between function and procedure

Answer:

Procedure can return zero or n values whereas function can return one value which is mandatory.

Procedures can have input/output parameters for it whereas functions can have only input parameters.

Procedure allows select as well as DML statement in it whereas function allows only select statement in it.

Functions can be called from procedure whereas procedures cannot be called from function.

Exception can be handled by try-catch block in a procedure whereas try-catch block cannot be used in a function.

We can go for transaction management in procedure whereas we can't go in function.

Procedures can not be utilized in a select statement whereas function can be embedded in a select statement.

UDF can be used in the SQL statements anywhere in the WHERE/

HAVING/SELECT section where as Stored procedures cannot be.

UDFs that return tables can be treated as another rowset. This can be used in JOINs with other tables.

Inline UDF's can be though of as views that take parameters and can be used in JOINs and other Rowsetoperations

Bottom of Form

Question 33: What is SQL loader

Answer:

SQL*Loader is a tool used by DBAs and developers to populate Oracle tables with data from flat files. The SQL*Loader gives a lot of flexibility to selectively load certain columns but not others, or to exclude certain records entirely. SQL*Loader has some advantages over programming languages that allow embedded SQL statements, as well. SQL*Loader consists of understanding its elements. The first is the data to be loaded, which is stored in the datafile (this is basically a flat/text file, and should not be confused with Oracle Server data files, that make up the database). The second is the control file (this is basically a text file, acting as a directive to the Loader, it should not be confused with Oracle Servers control file, which holds database-related information). SQL*Loader accepts special parameters that can affect how the load occurs, called command-line parameters. These parameters which include the ID (username/password or commonly know as the schema) to use while loading data, the name of the data file, and the name of the control file.

SQL*Loader in action consists of several additional items. If in the course of performing data loads, SQL*Loader encounters records it cannot load, the record is rejected and the SQL*Loader puts it in a special file called bad file. Additionally, SQL*Loader gives the user options to reject data based on special criteria. These criteria are defined in the control file as a part of the when clause. Is the SQL*Loader encounters a record that fails a specified when clause, the record is placed in a special file called discard file.

Question 34:.what is INSTR AND SUBSTR function

Substr

It allows you to extract a portion or subset of contiguous (connected) characters from a string. There are three arguments to it. In first argument the character string is given. In the second argument there the starting position id given from where the extraction should be started and in the third argument you provide the number of characters to be extracted.

SQL> select substr('Oracle',3,3) from dual;

SUB

—

acl

The INSTR function searches a string to find a match for the substring and, if found, returns the position, in the source string, of the first character of that substring. If there is no match, then INSTR returns 0.

First argument is a string, second argument is a string too, functions finds the string given in the second argument from the string given in the first argument. Third and fourth arguments are optional, in third argument we tell the function from what position of the string in the 1st argument search should start. Say the string in 2nd argument appears two or three times in the string in the 1st argument then the fourth argument tells which appearance to find.

SQL> select instr('Oracle Corporation','r',1,3) INSTR

2 from dual;

INSTR

Question 36: what is different between IN and Exists?

Answer: using the IN clause, you're telling the rule-based optimizer that you want the inner query to drive the outer query (think: IN = inside to outside).

When you write EXISTS in a where clause, you're telling the optimizer that you want the outer query to be run first, using each value to fetch a value from the inner query (think: EXISTS = outside to inside).

Question 37: what is the trigger?

Answer: Oracle lets you define procedures called triggers that run implicitly when an INSERT, UPDATE, or DELETE statement is issued against the associated table or, in some cases, against a view, or when database system actions occur. These procedures can be written in PL/SQL or Java and stored in the database, or they can be written as C callouts.

Triggers are similar to stored procedures.

Question 38.what is database links?

Answer: Database Links The central concept in distributed database systems is a database link. A database link is a connection between two physical database servers that allows a client to access them as one logical database.

Question 39. What are the packages?

Answer A package is a schema object that groups logically related

PL/SQL types, items, and subprograms. Packages usually have two parts, a specification, and a body, although sometimes the body is unnecessary. The specification (spec for short) is the interface to your applications; it declares the types, variables, constants, exceptions, cursors, and subprograms available for use. The body fully defines cursors and subprograms, and so implements the spec.

Question 40.what is the difference between %notfound and no data found

Answer NO DATA FOUND is an Exception whereas NOTFOUND is a cursor attribute

NO DATA FOUND: Is an exception which is raised when no rows are retrieved from the database in a SELECT statement

then PL/SQL raises the exception NO_DATA_FOUND.

Question 41. Find the nth highest salary from an employee table?

Answer: Co related sub query:

SELECT * FROM Employee Emp1

WHERE (N-1) = (SELECT COUNT(DISTINCT(Emp2.Salary))

FROM Employee Emp2 WHERE Emp2.Salary > Emp1.Salary)

Sybase / SQL server:

SELECT Top 1 Salary AS Salary FROM Employee WHERE SALARY IN (SELECT DISTINCT TOP 3 SALARY FROM Employee ORDER BY SALARY DESC) ORDER BY SALARY

My SQL: SELECT salary FROM (SELECT salary FROM Employee

ORDER BY salary DESC LIMIT 2) AS emp ORDER BY salary LIMIT 1;

SELECT * FROM (SELECT salary, first_name, row_number() over (order by salary) as rn

FROM employees) WHERE rn <= 3 ORDER BY salary;

Question 42: How to delete a duplicate record in a table?

Answer:Delete from employee where Rowid not in (Select min (Rowid) from employee group by Rowid)

delete from <table_name> where rowid not in   (select min(rowid)

from exp group by column1..,column2,...column3..);

Question 43. What is an ALIAS command?

ALIAS name can be given to a table or column. This alias name can be referred in WHERE clause to identify the table or column.

Question 44. What is the difference between TRUNCATE and DROP statements?

TRUNCATE removes all the rows from the table, and it cannot be rolled back. DROP command removes a table from the database and operation cannot be rolled back.

Question 45. What are aggregate and scalar functions?

Aggregate functions are used to evaluate mathematical calculation and return single values. This can be calculated from the columns in a table. Scalar functions return a single value based on the input value.

Example -.

Aggregate – max(), count – Calculated with respect to numeric.

Scalar – UCASE(), NOW() – Calculated with respect to strings.

Question 46 How can you create an empty table from an existing table?

An example will be -. Select * into studentcopy from student where 1=2.

Here, we are copying student table to another table with the same structure with no rows copied.

Question 47 How to fetch alternate records from a table?

Records can be fetched for both Odd and Even row numbers -.

To display even numbers-.Select studentId from (Select rowno, studentId from student) where mod(rowno,2)=0.

Select studentId from (Select rowno, studentId from student) where mod(rowno,2)=0.

To display odd numbers-.1Select studentId from (Select rowno, studentId from student) where mod(rowno,2)=1.

Question 48. How to select unique records from a table?

Select unique records from a table by using the DISTINCT keyword.

Select DISTINCT StudentID, StudentName from Student.

Question 49. What is the command used to fetch first 5 characters of the string?

There are many ways to fetch first 5 characters of the string -.

Select SUBSTRING(StudentName,1,5) as studentname from student.

Select RIGHT(Studentname,5) as studentname from student.

Question 50: What are components of SQL?

Answer: Data Definition Language (DDL): It's a set of SQL commands used to create modify and delete database structures but not the data.DDL manages table and index structure. The most basic items of DDL are CREATE, ALTER, RENAME, DROP and TRUNCATE statements:

CREATE creates an object (a table, for example) in the database, e.g.:

CREATE TABLE My_table(my_field1 INT, my_field2 VARCHAR(50), my_field3 DATE NOT NULL, PRIMARY KEY (my_field1, my_field2));

ALTER modifies the structure of an existing object in various ways, for example, adding a column to an existing table or a constraint, e.g.:

ALTER TABLE My_table ADD my_field4 NUMBER(3) NOT NULL;

TRUNCATE deletes all data from a table in a very fast way, deleting the data inside the table and not the table itself. It usually implies a subsequent COMMIT operation, i.e., it cannot be rolled back (data is not written to the logs for rollback later, unlike DELETE).

TRUNCATE TABLE My_table;

DROP deletes an object in the database, usually irretrievably, i.e., it cannot be rolled back, e.g.:

DROP TABLE My_table;

Data manipulation The Data Manipulation Language (DML) is the subset of SQL used to add, update and delete data:

INSERT adds rows (formally tuples) to an existing table, e.g.:

INSERT INTO My_table (field1, field2, field3)

VALUES ('test', 'N', NULL);

UPDATE modifies a set of existing table rows, e.g.:

UPDATE My_table SET field1 = 'updated value' WHERE field2 = 'N';

DELETE removes existing rows from a table, e.g.:

DELETE FROM My_table WHERE field2 = 'N';

MERGE is used to combine the data of multiple tables. It combines the INSERT and UPDATE elements.

MERGE INTO TABLE_NAME USING table_reference ON (condition)

WHEN MATCHED THEN

UPDATE SET column1 = value1 [, column2 = value2 ...]

WHEN NOT MATCHED THEN

INSERT (column1 [, column2 ...]) VALUES (value1 [, value2 ...])

Transaction controls: It is a component of SQL statement that controls access to data. Transactions, if available, wrap DML operations:

START TRANSACTION (or BEGIN WORK, or BEGIN TRANSACTION, depending on SQL dialect) marks the start of a database transaction, which either completes entirely or not at all.

SAVE TRANSACTION (or SAVEPOINT) saves the state of the database at the current point in the transaction

CREATE TABLE tbl_1(id INT);

INSERT INTO tbl_1(id) VALUES(1);

INSERT INTO tbl_1(id) VALUES(2);

COMMIT;

UPDATE tbl_1 SET id=200 WHERE id=1;

SAVEPOINT id_1upd;

UPDATE tbl_1 SET id=1000 WHERE id=2;

ROLLBACK TO id_1upd;

SELECT id FROM tbl_1;

COMMIT causes all data changes in a transaction to be made permanent.

ROLLBACK causes all data changes since the last COMMIT or ROLLBACK to be discarded, leaving the state of the data as it was prior to those changes.

Once the COMMIT statement completes, the transaction's changes cannot be rolled back.

COMMIT and ROLLBACK terminate the current transaction and release data locks. In the absence of a START TRANSACTION or similar statement, the semantics of SQL are implementation-dependent. The following example shows a classic transfer of funds transaction, where money is removed from one account and added to another. If either the removal or the addition fails, the entire transaction is rolled back.

START TRANSACTION;

UPDATE Account SET amount=amount-200 WHERE account_number=1234;

UPDATE Account SET amount=amount+200 WHERE account_number=2345;

IF ERRORS=0 COMMIT;

IF ERRORS<>0 ROLLBACK;

UNIX INTERVIEW QUESTIONS

These are real interview questions and very useful.

What is UNIX

Unix is an Operating system a family of multitasking, multiuser computer operating systems.

Many of the proprietary flavors have been designed to run only (or mainly) on proprietary hardware sold by the same company that has developed them. Examples include:

AIX – developed by IBM for use on its mainframe computers

BSD/OS – a commercial version of BSD developed by Wind River for Intel processors

HP-UX – developed by Hewlett-Packard for its HP 9000 series of business servers

IRIX – developed by SGI for applications that use 3-D visualization and virtual reality

QNX – a real-time operating system developed by QNX Software Systems primarily for use in embedded systems

Solaris – developed by Sun Microsystems for the SPARC platform and the most widely used proprietary flavor for web servers

Tru64 – developed by Compaq for the Alpha processor

Others are developed by groups of volunteers who make them available for free. Among them are:

Linux – the most popular and fastest-growing of all the Unix-like operating systems

Question 1: How to check a Job (Status) or Process in Unix.

Answer: Command is given below

ps –ef | grep jobname

if it gives no result then it means job complete successful

Also if you want to check the last command was successfully completed in Unix or its status

echo $? Is 0 means successful completed else not

Question 2: How to check Crontab scheduling?

Answer. Crontab –e

Now there are 5 entries you set and gave the filename /command that needs to execute at the scheduled time.

Minute	Hour	Day of Month	Month	Day of Week	Command
# (0-59)	(0-23)	(1-31)	(1-12 or Jan-Dec)	(0-6 or Sun-Sat)	

Question 3: How to remove white lines?

Answer:

sed '/^$/d' myfile should delete the blank lines

grep -v '^$' file_name > file_name

Question 4: the difference between xargs and exec?

Answer: both commands are almost similar but they have different results.

find . -name H* -exec ls -l {} \; executes the command ls -l on each individual file.

find . -name H* | xargs ls -l constructs an argument list from the output of the find command and passes it to ls.

consider if the output of the find command produced:

H1

H2

H3

the first command would execute

ls -l H1

ls -l H2

ls -l H3

but the second would execute

ls -l H1 H2 H3

find /home/ganesh -type d | xargs chmod 755 and to accomplish steps #2 and #4 together.

find /home/ganesh -type d -exec chmod 755 {} ;

Question 5. What is Mail command

Answer: mailx -s"test" -r email@domain.com < uuencodefile

Question 6. Difference between types of Shells?

Answer.

Bourne-It is available on all UNIX systems. This shell does not have the interactive facilities provided by modern shells such as the C shell and Korn shell.

c shell- it allows aliasing command. Command history

Korn shell-Superset of bourne shell

Question 7: How to check no of users login in Unix.

Answer:

$who

$whoami

$id

Question 8: How to check Unix version

Answer:$ uname -r

Question 9: How to check the file system

Answer:$fsck

Question 10: What is the default permission of any file and dir in Unix? umask command?

Answer: 666

644 File permission

777 dir permission

we can change the default permission by using umask

Question 11: How to list hidden file

Answer: ls -a

Question 12:.what is sticky bit?

Answer: Sticky bit set then only owner or superuser can rename or delete the file.

sticky bit is a user ownership access-right flag that can be assigned to files and directories on Unix systems

The sticky bit can be set using the chmod command and can be set using its octal mode 1000 or by its symbol t (s is already used by the setuid bit). For example, to add the bit on the directory /usr/local/tmp, one would type chmod +t /usr/local/tmp. Or, to make sure that directory has standard tmp permissions, one could also type chmod 1777 /usr/local/tmp.

To clear it, use chmod -t /usr/local/tmp or chmod 0777 /usr/local/tmp (using numeric mode will also change directory tmp to standard permissions).

In Unix symbolic file system permission notation, the sticky bit is represented by the letter t in the final character-place. For instance, on Solaris 8, the /tmp directory, which by default has the sticky-bit set, shows up as:

$ ls -ld /tmp

drwxrwxrwt 4 root   sys   485 Nov 10 06:01 /tmp

If the sticky-bit is set on a file or directory without the execution bit set for the others category (non-user-owner and non-group-owner), it is indicated with a capital T:

ls -l test

-rw-r–r– 1 root   other   0 Nov 10 12:57 test

chmod +t test; ls -l test

-rw-r–r-T 1 root   other   0 Nov 10 12:57 test

Question 13.How to identify an executable file in unix

Answer: grep -r xxxx "."

find . -type f \(-perm -u=x -o -perm -g=x -o -perm -o=x \)

grep -r xxxx *.*

Question 14: Print the dir only in Unix

Answer: ls -l | grep '^d'

Question 15: what is the diff between df and du

Answer: du is disk space used by file sys. df is disk space free

du == Disk Usage. It walks through a directory tree and counts the sum size of all files therein. It may not output exact information due to the possibility of unreadable files, hard links in the directory tree, etc. It will show information about the specific directory requested. Think, "How much disk space is being used by these files?"

df == Disk Free. Looks at disk used blocks directly in filesystem metadata. Because of this, it returns much faster that du but can only show info about the entire disk/partition. Think, "How much free disk space do I have?"

df -h /tmp

Output:

Filesystem   Size   Used   Avail Capacity Mounted on

/dev/ad0s1e 496M   22M   434M   5%   /tmp

Now type du command:

du -d 0 -h /tmp/

Output:

22M   /tmp/

Question 16:List the file on the basis of their size (in ascending order)

Answer:ls -l|awk '{print $5,$9|"sort -n"}'

Question 17: how to find the latest file with a timestamp

Answer: now=`date +%Y%m`

ls -rt filename_"$now"*.csv | tail | read file

cp $file standard_file_name

Question 18: How can we change the access time of a file

Answer: touch filename

Question 19. Remove the duplicate the file

Answer: $sort -u filename

Question 20.what is the system calls in Unix

Answer: A request for the OS to do something on behalf of the users' program. System calls are function used in kernel itself. Unix syscalls are used to manage the file system to control process and to provide interprocess comm.

open()

close()

chmod()

read()

kill()

fork()

exec()

Question 21. What is fork? what is zombie process? how to kill a zombie process?

Answer: fork: a system call that creates a new process under the UNIX operating system

When a program forks and the child finishes before the parent, the kernel still keeps some of its information about the child in case the parent might need it — for example, the parent may need to check the child's exit status. To be able to get this information, the parent calls wait(); when this happens, the kernel can discard the information.

In the interval between the child terminating and the parent calling wait(), the child is said to be a `zombie'. (If you do `ps', the child will have a `Z' in its status field to indicate this.) Even though it's not running, it's still taking up an entry in the process table. (It consumes no other resources, but some utilities may show bogus figures for e.g. CPU usage; this is because some parts of the process table entry have been overlaid by accounting info to save space.)

you can kill a zombie process by killing the parent process. this is done by issuing

kill -18 PPID or by rebooting your system

will clean up any zombie process.

It can be killed with normal kill -9 command also

Question 22. How to change a background process to foreground?

Answer: $fg %job id or $fg #PID

Question 23.how can we search string in file? grep -e,i,c,f,v stands for (grep -e?, grep -f- fixed)

Answer: grep "text" test.sh > test1.sh

Question 24 .how to find file name contains a particular string?

Answer: find .-type f | xargs grep string

xargs breaks the list of arguments into sublists small enough to be acceptable.

Question 25. How to print the fifth field in unix using awk,cut

Answer : awk -f " '{print $5}' filename
cut -d " f5 filename

AWK is an excellent tool for processing these rows and columns and is easier to use AWK than most conventional programming languages. It can be considered to be a pseudo-C interpreter, as it under

Question 27. What is the command line parameter? how many we can use

Answer: Command-Line Arguments:

The command-line arguments $1, $2, $3,...$9 are positional parameters, with $0 pointing to the actual command, program, shell script, or function and $1, $2, $3, ...$9 as the arguments to the command.

Following script uses various special variables related to the command line:

Question 28. What is the meaning of top most line in any unix shell script?(ask)

#!/bin/ksh

Answer:If it finds an exclamation point (!), or Bang!, as it's known, then what follows is taken as the path to the shell executable binary program. Not only that, but all the command line arguments that the shell executable allows can also be stacked up on this line

Question 29.what is shell?

Answer: A program that interprets the users request and gives the response of req to users

Question 30.What is the use of Nice command?

Answer: executes a command with updated scheduling priority

Question31: What is the diff between egrep ,fgrep,grep

Answer: fgrep= fixed grep

Egrep: extended grep

gerp Search a Pattern from the current directory.

egrep (grep -E in linux) is extended grep where additional regular expression meta characters have been added like +, ?, | and ().

fgrep (grep -F in linux) is fixed or fast grep and behaves as grep but does not recognize any regular expression meta characters as being special

Question32. what is inode number?

Answer: inode (index node) is a data structure found in many Unix file systems. Each inode stores all the information about a file system object (file, device node, socket,pipe, etc.), except data content and file name

Question 33: how can we change env variable

Answer:Display env variable $set

set mail=/usr/mail/vivek

Following are most command examples of environment variables used under UNIX operating systems:

PATH – Display lists directories the shell searches, for the commands.

HOME – User's home directory to store files.

TERM – Set terminal emulator being used by UNIX.

PS1 – Display shell prompt in the Bourne shell and variants.

MAIL – Path to user's mailbox.

TEMP – Path to where processes can store temporary files.

JAVA_HOME – Sun (now Oracle) JDK path.

ORACLE_HOME – Oracle database installation path.

TZ – Timezone settings

PWD – Path to the current directory.

HISTFILE – The name of the file in which command history is saved

HISTFILESIZE -The maximum number of lines contained in the

history file

HOSTNAME -The system's host name

LD_LIBRARY_PATH -It is a colon-separated set of directories where libraries should be searched for.

USER -Current logged in user's name.

DISPLAY -Network name of the X11 display to connect to, if available.

SHELL -The current shell.

TERMCAP – Database entry of the terminal escape codes to perform various terminal functions.

OSTYPE – Type of operating system.

MACHTYPE – The CPU architecture that the system is running on.

EDITOR – The user's a preferred text editor.

PAGER – The user's preferred text pager.

MANPATH – Colon separated list of directories to search for manual pages.

Question34: how to list files as per their size

Answer: ls -l|awk '{print $5,$9|"sort -n"}'

Question 35.how to copy and paste is vi editor

Answer: 1. Move the cursor to the first line to be copied.

> 2. '4yy'

> 3. Move the cursor to the destination.

> 4. 'p'

Question 36: VI queries

how to delete a line in vi

Answer: In command mode,

dd deletes the line where the cursor is

how to replace a string in vi?

Answer: In command mode

cc cw etc

In escape mode

:s | ptn1 | ptn2

how to search a string in vi?

Answer: command mode

/pattern-searches fwd

?pattern-searches backward

Question 37.How to replace a string using sed command

sed -i 's/old-word/new-word/g' *.txt

Question 38. How to replace a character in a file using translate

cat filename | tr "old char" "new char"

#sed 'ADDRESSs/REGEXP/REPLACEMENT/FLAGS' filename

#sed 'PATTERNs/REGEXP/REPLACEMENT/FLAGS' filename

s is substitute command

/ is a delimiter

REGEXP is regular expression to match

REPLACEMENT is a value to replace

FLAGS can be any of the following

g Replace all the instance of REGEXP with REPLACEMENT

n Could be any number,replace nth instance of the REGEXP with REPLACEMENT.

p If substitution was made, then prints the new pattern space.

i match REGEXP in a case-insensitive manner.

w file If substitution was made, write out the result to the given file.

We can use different delimiters (one of @ % ; :) instead of /

Question 39How to print 100-110 lines in Unix

Answer : $Head -110 | tail +100

sed -n '100,110p' input.file > output.file

Question 40.what is $?,$#,$* in Unix

Answer : $?- tells the exit status of last exec command

$#- tells the no of command line args

$*-contains entire string of args

Question 41.how to move a file from one system to another?

Answer: Remote copy: Rcp copies files between machines. Each file or directory argument is either a remote file name of the form "rname@rhost:path", or a local file name (containing no `:' characters, or a ` /' before any `:'s).

rcp -r zeus.univ.edu:backups/documents study

Question 42.how to send a mail in unix with attachement?

Answer:(cat body.txt

uuencode pic.jpg pic.jpg

) | mailx -s "subject" abc@xyz.com

Question 43.how to check CPU Utilization?

Answer: $top

sar : System activity reporter

=> mpstat : Report per-processor or per-processor-set statistics

=> ps / top commands

Question 44: list files that accessed in last 30 days and remove them

Answer: find /mydir -atime +30 -exec rm {} \;

Question 45. what is the background process in oracle

Answer:

PMON

SMON

CKPT

DBWR

LGWR

ARCH

Question 46.what is the daemon process in Unix

Answer: In Unix and other computer multitasking operating systems, a daemon is a computer program that runs in the background, rather than under the direct control of a user; they are usually initiated as background processes.

Question 47.how to change group of a file

$ chown username:usergroup somefile

Question 48.what is the tar command used for to generate achived tape

Answer: tar command is short for tape archiving. To combine multiple files and/or directories into a single file, use the following command:

tar -cvf file.tar inputfile1 inputfile2

Replace inputfile1 and inputfile2 with the files and/or directories you want to combine. You can use any name in place of file.tar, though you should keep the .tar extension. If you don't use the f option, tar assumes you really do want to create a tape archive instead of joining up a number of files. The v option tells tar to be verbose, which reports all files as they are added.

To separate an archive created by tar into separate files, at the shell prompt, enter:

tar -xvf file.tar

Compressing and uncompressing tar files

Many modern Unix systems, such as Linux, use GNU tar, a version of tar produced by the Free Software Foundation. If your system uses GNUtar, you can easily use gzip (the GNU file compression program) in conjunction with tar to create compressed archives. To do this, enter:

tar -cvzf file.tar.gz inputfile1 inputfile2

Here, the z option tells tar to zip the archive as it is created. To unzip such a zipped tar file, enter:

tar -xvzf file.tar.gz

Alternatively, if your system does not use GNU tar, but nonetheless does have gzip, you can still create a compressed tar file, via the following command:

tar -cvf – inputfile1 inputfile2 | gzip > file.tar.gz

Note: If gzip isn't available on your system, use the Unix compress command instead. In the example above, replace gzip with compress and change the .gz extension to .Z (the compress command specifically looks for an uppercase Z). You can use other compression programs in this way as well. Just be sure to use the appropriate extension for the compressed file, so you can identify which program to use to decompress the file later.

If you are not using GNU tar, to separate a tar archive that was compressed by gzip, enter:

gunzip -c file.tar.gz | tar -xvf –

Similarly, to separate a tar archive compressed with the Unix compress command, replace gunzip with uncompress .

Lastly, the extensions .tgz and .tar.gz are equivalent; they both signify a tar file zipped with gzip.

Question 49.difference between kill and kill -9

Answer Kill command is use to send signal to a process or to kill a process. We typically use kill -SIGNAL PID, where you know the PID of the process.

The kill command causes the specified signal to be sent to the specified process. The kill command has the general form as follows:

kill -N PID

Where,

N is a signal number

PID is the Process Identification Number. If you do not know the PID, it can be learned through the ps command.

§ The signal number 1 is a hangup signal. I recommended using 1 signal because it should kill the process and it can save the buffer (if supported). For example if it is an editor, save the buffer. This is the default if you do not specify a signal number. Signal number 9, a kill signal, is the surest way to kill a process.

§ Some of the more commonly used signals:

signal #   Usage

1   HUP (hang up)

2   INT (interrupt)

3   QUIT (quit)

6   ABRT (abort)

9   KILL (non-catchable, non-ignorable kill)

14   ALRM (alarm clock)

15   TERM (software termination signal)

Question 50: How to add one field in the last line of a file

Answer:

to add a line at beginning of the file

sed '1 i this is first line' file

to add at end of file

```
sed '$ a this is last line' file
```

AUTOSYS JOB SCHEDULING INTERVIEW QUESTIONS

Autosys is one of the important job scheduling tools and widely used in banks. Here I am sharing interview questions related to Autosys tools.

Question1: What is autosys? Why do we need to use autosys?

Answer: AutoSys is used for defining, scheduling, and monitoring jobs. These jobs can be a UNIX script, java program or any other program which can be invoked from the shell. Before starting we assume that the user has already set up an AutoSys environment. This environment consists of autosys server and client.

AutoSys System components

1. Event server (AutoSys database)

2. Event processor

3. Remote agent

Event Server

The event server is a AutoSys database which stores all system information and events as well as all job, monitor and report definitions. Sometimes this database is also called as a data server, which actually describes a server instance. That is, it is either a UNIX or Windows process, and it is associated with data space (or raw disk storage), that can include multiple databases or tablespaces.

Event Processor

This is the main component of the autosys system. This processes all the events it reads from data server. The event processor is the program, running either as a UNIX process or as a Windows service that actually runs AutoSys. It schedules and starts jobs. When you start the event processor it continually scans the database for events to be processed. When it finds one, it checks whether the event satisfies the starting conditions for any job in the database.

Remote Agent

On a UNIX machine, the remote agent is a temporary process started by the event processor to perform a specific task on a remote (client) machine. On a Windows machine, the remote agent is a Windows service running on a remote (client) machine that is directed by the event processor to perform specific tasks.

The remote agent starts the command specified for a given job, sends running and completion information about a task to the event server, then exits. If the remote agent is unable to transfer the information, it waits and tries again until it can successfully communicate with the database.

Basic functionality of AutoSys

Below is the diagram which explains the basic functionality, please check the explanation.

1. The event processor scans the event server for the next event to process. If no event is ready, the event processor scans again in five seconds.

2. The event processor reads from the event server that an event is ready. If the event is a STARTJOB event, the job definition and attributes are retrieved from the Event Server, including the command and the pointer (full path name on the client machine) to the profile file to be used for the job. In addition, for jobs running on Windows machines, the event processor retrieves from the database the user IDs and passwords required to run the job on the client machine.

3. The event processor processes the event. If the event is a STARTJOB, the event processor attempts to establish a connection with the remote agent on the client machine, and passes the job attributes to the client machine.

The event processor sends a CHANGE_STATUS event marking in the event server that the job is in STARTING state.

4. On a UNIX machine, the inetd invokes the remote agent. On a Windows machine, the remote agent logs onto the machine as the user defined as the job's owner, using the user IDs and passwords passed to it from the event processor.

5. The remote agent sends an acknowledgment back to the event processor indicating that it has received the job parameters. The socket connection is terminated. At this point, the event processor resumes scanning the event server database, looking for events to process.

6. The remote agent starts a process and executes the command in the job definition.

7. The remote agent issues a CHANGE_STATUS event marking in the event server that the job is in RUNNING state.

8. The client job process runs to completion, then returns an exit code to the remote agent and quits.

Question 3: how to define autosys job?

Answer: There are various parameters to define autosys job. Starting from the profile, timezone, start time, starting condition and so on. There are the two methods you can use to create job definitions:

1. Using the AutoSys Graphical User Interface (GUI).

2. Using the AutoSys Job Information Language (JIL) through a command-line interface.

L stands for Job Information Language. Using this you can instruct autosys to save job definitions. This information saved in autosys database. You can also create a jil file which contains job definition. You can then pass this jil file to autosys.

Essential attributes for defining job

1. Job Name

JIL Keyword : insert_job. Name used to identify the job.

2. Job Type

a. JIL Keyword : job_type. The job type is one of job types: command (c), file watcher (f) or box (b).

3. Owner

a. JIL Keyword : owner

The job owner specifies whose user ID the command will be run under on the client machine. This attribute is automatically set to the user who invoked jil or the GUI to define the job, and cannot be changed except by the edit superuser.

Other job attributes:

1. command: The command attribute can be the name of any command, executable, UNIX shell script or batch file, and its arguments.

2. machine: This attribute specifies the client machine on which the command should be run.

3. date_condition: The start date/time dependencies attribute is a toggle, which specifies whether or not there are date, time, or both, conditions required for starting the job.

4. days_of_week: The days of the week attribute specifies the days on which the job should be run.

Sample jil file for command job echoJob.jil

insert_job:echoJob

machine:unixMachine

owner:username

command:echo "Hello this is command job"

To add this job in atosys db. Run the following command from unix:

jil < echoJob.jil

This command will add "echoJob" job to autosys database.

Question 3: Types of jobs in Autosys?

Answer: There are three types of jobs: command, file watcher, and box.

As their names imply, command jobs execute commands, box jobs are containers that hold other jobs (including other boxes), and file watcher jobs watch for the arrival of a specified file. In the AutoSys environment, the box job (or box) is a container of other jobs. A box job can be used to organize and control process flow. The box itself performs no actions, although it can trigger other jobs to run. An important feature of this type of job is that boxes can be put inside of other boxes.

Default Box Job Behavior: Some important rules to remember about boxes are

Jobs run only once per box execution.

Jobs in a box will start only if the box itself is running.

As long as any job in a box is running, the box remains in a RUNNING state; the box cannot complete until all jobs have run.

By default, a box will return a status of SUCCESS only when all the jobs in the box have run and the status of all the jobs is "success.

By default, a box will return a status of FAILURE only when all jobs in the box have run and the status of one or more of the jobs is "failure."

Unless otherwise specified, a box will run indefinitely until it reaches a status of SUCCESS or FAILURE.

Changing the state of a box to INACTIVE (via the send event command) changes the state of all the jobs in the box to INACTIVE.

Question: What is the status of Autosys Job?

Answer: Following are the status of Autosys jobs

INACTIVE : The job has not yet been processed. Either the job has never been run, or its status was intentionally altered to "turn off" its previous completion status

ACTIVATED :The top-level box that this job is in is now in the RUNNING state, but the job itself has not started yet.

STARTING : The event processor has initiated the start job procedure with the Remote Agent.

RUNNING : The job is running. If the job is a box job, this value simply means that the jobs within the box may be started (other conditions permitting). If it is a command or file watcher job, the value means that the process is actually running on the remote machine.

SUCCESS : The job exited with an exit code equal to or less than the "maximum exit code for success." By default, only the exit code "0" is interpreted as "success." If the job is a box job, this value means that all the jobs within the box have finished with the status SUCCESS (the default), or the "Exit Condition for Box Success" evaluated to true

FAILURE : The job exited with an exit code greater than the "maximum exit code for success." By default, any number greater than zero is interpreted as "failure." AutoSys issues an alarm if a job fails

TERMINATED : The job terminated while in the RUNNING state. A job can be terminated if a user sends a KILLJOB event or if it was defined to terminate if the box it is in failed. If the job itself fails, it has a FAILURE status, not a TERMINATED status. A job may also be terminated if it has exceeded the maximum run time (term_run_time attribute, if one was specified for the job), or if it was killed from the command line through a UNIX kill command. AutoSys issues an alarm if a job is terminated.

RESTART : The job was unable to start due to hardware or application problems, and has been scheduled to restart.

QUE_WAIT : The job can logically run (that is, all the starting conditions have been met), but there are not enough machine resources available.

ON_HOLD : This job is on hold and will not be run until it receives the JOB_OFF_HOLD event.

ON_ICE : This job is removed from all conditions and logic, but is still defined to AutoSys. Operationally, this condition is like deactivating the job. It will remain on ice until it receives the JOB_OFF_ICE event.

Question: What is the difference between ON HOLD AND ON ICE:

Answer:The difference between "on hold" and "on ice" is that when an "on hold" job is taken off hold, if its starting conditions are already satisfied, it will be scheduled to run, and it will run. On the other hand, if an "on ice" job is taken "off ice," it will not start, even if its starting conditions are already satisfied. This job will not run until its starting conditions reoccur.

The other major distinction is that jobs downstream from the job that is "on ice" will run as though the job succeeded. Whereas, all dependent jobs do not run when a job is on "on hold"—nothing downstream from this job will run.

Question: What are the starting parameters for Autosys parameters?

Answer: Starting Parameters: AutoSys determines whether to start or not to start a job based on the evaluation of the starting conditions (or starting parameters) defined for the job. These conditions can be one or more of the following:

¦ Date and time scheduling parameters are met (it is or has passed the specified date and time).

¦ Starting Conditions specified in the job definition evaluate to true.

¦ For jobs in a box, the box must be in the RUNNING state.

¦ The current status of the job is not ON_HOLD or ON_ICE.

Question: How to write JIL code?

Answer: sample jil code / Writing jil code:

jil = Job information language

When using JIL to create a job definition, you enter the jil command to display the JIL prompt.

Runs the Job Information Language (JIL) processor to add, update, and delete AutoSys jobs, machines, monitors, and reports. Also used to insert one-time job override definitions.

/* ——————— SAP_UAT_MU03_C ——————— */

insert_job: SAP_UAT_MU03_C job_type: c

command: /local/SAP/processCheckUAT.sh

machine: MU03-UAT

owner: admin@MU03-UAT

permission: gx,wx,mx,me

days_of_week: all

start_times: "15:00, 14:00"

description: "Job used for Run testing of process"

alarm_if_fail: 1

max_exit_success: 1

____

—-

The above example is a simple jil code of autosys which we have to write if we want any particular job to be thru autosys.

To Insert a new JIL code :

issue command "jil"

bash-3.00$ jiljil>>1>

"The following prompt will appear" copy paste the jil code u have made example of jil code below………..

At the end the "C" or "B" determines if the job is box job or child job.

if the jil is inserted properly successfull message will come if any errors are there the jil code contains some errors..

if successfull exit;

2. Other way is to create a temp file named temp.jil which contains jil code on autosys server: give command.

bash-3.00$ jil<>

Question : Please list all autosys command?

Answer: Functional Listing of AutoSys Commands :

Accessing Sybase : xql

Checking System Status : autoflags

autoping

autosyslog

chase chk_auto_up

Converting cron to JIL (UNIX Only) : cron2jil

Defining AutoSys Jobs or Machines : jil

Defining Calendars : autocal, autocal_asc

Reporting Job Status : autorep

autostatus

Starting AutoSys (UNIX Only) : eventor

Stopping AutoSys : sendevent

Using Autorep command:

Function

Reports information about a job, jobs within boxes, machines, and machine status. Also reports information about job overrides and global variables.

autorep {-J job_name -M machine_name -G global_name} [-s -d -q -o over_num] [-r run_num]

autorep -J (job name here)

This will display a list of jobs with complete details with box/jobname, last/latest run date & time, status, exit code, etc.

Viewing JIL code for any Autosys job

autorep -J (job name here) -q

To obtain the underlying JIL (Job Interaction Language) source code for any Autosys job, run command:

To obtain the information of previous runs

autorep -J (job name here) -r (No of runs back) example : autorep -J (job name here) -r 1

would generate a report for the job run one runs back

—

Status Abbreviations

The following table lists the abbreviations used in the ST (status) column of the autorep report, and gives the status for each abbreviation.

AC – ACTIVATED

FA – FAILURE

IN – INACTIVE

OH – ON_HOLD

OI – ON_ICE

QU – QUE_WAIT

RE – RESTART

RU – RUNNING

ST – STARTING

SU – SUCCESS

TE – TERMINATED

sendevent: sendevents to AutoSys for a variety of purposes, including starting or stopping AutoSys jobs, stopping the Event processor, and putting a job on hold. This command is also used to set AutoSys global variables or cancel a scheduled event.

sendevent is normally used with "-E" & -J option

-J job_name : Specifies the name of the job to which the specified event should be sent. This option is required for all events except STOP_DEMON, COMMENT, ALARM, or SET_GLOBAL

-E event :Specifies the event to be sent. This option is required. Any one of the following events may be specified:

STARTJOB

KILLJOB

DELETEJOB

FORCE_STARTJOB

JOB_ON_ICE

JOB_OFF_ICE

JOB_ON_HOLD

JOB_OFF_HOLD

CHANGE_STATUS

STOP_DEMON

CHANGE_PRIORITY

COMMENT

ALARM

SET_GLOBAL

SEND_SIGNAL

Following are the example of sendevent command frequently used.

To start or force start a job manually using sendevent :

sendevent –E FORCE_STARTJOB -J "Job Name Here"

sendevent -E STARTJOB -J "Job Name Here"

To put jobs on OFF ICE or ON ICE :

sendevent -E OFF_ICE -J "Job Name Here"

sendevent -E ON_ICE -J "Job Name Here"

autostatus: Reports the current status of a specific job, or the value of an AutoSys global variable. Ex: autostatus -J job_name, -S

AKHILENDRA VERMA

instance